Love, Laughs, an
Everyone's St
This is mine.

<u>CHAPTER 1</u>

Where do you start? At what point do you know what you want to write about?   Did the great novelists like D.H. Lawrence, James Boyce, and F. Scott Fitzgerald sit with their quill in hand hovering above their bright white sheet of A4 knowing, or having any idea what was going to be transferred from their grey matter onto the aforementioned canvas before them? Probably but, hey?   I am no novelist. Nor a Biographer, auto or otherwise.

So, what I propose to do, in a way that you can understand what sort of life I have enjoyed and endured,   is to write down, with the help of my Lady Donna and my Family and Friends, are the funniest situations, quotes, ironic and quite unbelievable happenings in my life.. So far. *"Why would I want to read the story of an everyday guy"* I hear the readers voice asks… well!   Maybe you can relate to the story as you are probably another `everyday guy` who is fed up to the back teeth, (or gums if you have dental phobia), of not being able to express yourself, either through, What ??   Nobody to talk to? An inferiority complex? Not being able to write it down because you are an illiterate bastard (Mind you, if you are, you probably cannot read this anyway. Get your Mammy to read it to you. But, then again, you have been spawned from the illiterate) If so, it is not too late to learn.

So, Where to start? Let us start away back on a cold winter's night at Barshaw Hospital in Paisley, Renfrewshire, Scotland at 01.20 a.m. on the 25th of January, in the year of

Our Lord 1953... (Rabbie Burns' day)
"WHAAH...! WHAAH...! WHAAH!!" the
first screaming vocals of one, Cornelius
O`Gormley Junior. These `vocals` (once
tuned) were to stand him in good stead later
in his life.   This was the seventh child of
Cornelius & Norah O'Gormley. Also, the
fourth Son.   Siblings who had arrived
before him were, Joseph, Mary, Kathleen,
Thomas, Daniel and Norah. (There were
another six to follow Cornelius Junior)
They being Christopher, Brian, Anthony,
Theresa, Patrick and Angela.

Some people
claim to remember early memories from
their childhood like `getting their `nappy`
changed.....I don't think so! Surely, that is
pushing it. I can remember wee things like
my Mum & older sisters playing `skipping-
ropes` with the neighbours on, what seemed
to be always sunny-days.
My Dad, with his Green uniform, Driving
Buses for the Glasgow Corporation and

giving Mum his `Pay-pack` on a Thursday evening. Waiting for his pocket money (or Guinness vouchers as he called them) so as to reward himself down at the local pub for his hard week of working. (In addition, he deserved it)

I can remember other bit's and pieces like Mum carrying me over to `switch` off the telly. A wee corner switch at the side of one of the first TV. Sets you could buy. A wee brown box with a bulbous screen. I don't know how we managed to afford one, but methinks it was because my wonderful Dad had this sort of inquisitive nature to find, and try out all things `new` or `modern`. When he was 12 years old for example, he got a Christmas or Birthday present of a Train-set, (a much sought-after item in the early 1930s) He loved, and indeed, enjoyed this much envied   toy but, he met a friend who had been given for his annual celebration, (birthday or Christmas) a

`Brownie Camera`. This `friend` was so disappointed with this `gadget`, he said to my Dad, *"I hate this thing! What do I want with a daft camera?"* My Dad must have had some insight into the possibilities of photography, or maybe he just got fed-up with watching his `train` going round and round, that he offered his friend a `swap`. His friend happily agreed to the transaction (obviously thinking my Dad was off his head) and so, my Dad started his `lifetime` hobby of photography. He was later to go further afield into `cine-cameras` (early camcorders to you and me)

Getting back to `having a telly`, we were indeed the first family to own a television on the street where we lived. Our house was, some nights, akin to a picture-hall (the pictures) with neighbours coming up to the house, just before `Sunday night at the London Palladium` started, with little `excuses` to my Mum like, *"Hi Norah, I made too many* *wee scones tonight. Ah thought mah sister wiz cumin` fur a wee visit but she canny make it. D`yi mind?”.* “b`jacus” Mum would say (b`jacus being a pseudonym for `be Jesus` as my Mum never `took the Lord's name in vain`) *“In ye come…oi don't know where yi goanna sit fur we got Mr `n` Mrs Martin, Mr `n` Mrs Markie, Mr `n` Mrs McBride, Mrs Harper, Mrs Black and her boys in here, as well as my lot” ..And we got a helluva lot o Scones”.* However, my Mum drew the line when `*The One O'clock Gang*` was on.

I look back at times and wonder how Mum and Dad managed to bring up 13 kids with no Government help. No Benefits or Housing allowance Dad worked hard all his life as did Mum. (In-between having Children) I can remember Mum doing a washing in the Bathtub, which included bedding as in Blankets and Sheets. Imagine the weight of a wet Blanket. She would then take it all outside to the backcourt and hang it all up to dry. I also remember Mum getting up early Morning to start up the Coal fire so us kids would get up to a nice warm house   to get ready for School.

One time my Dad was suffering from a sore back but insisted in still going to work against Mum's wishes. Dad could not bend down to tie his shoe laces and asked Mum to tie them for him. She refused so as he would take a day off work but, Dad just went to work anyway, with his shoe laces untied.

My Lovely Mum and Dad were devout Catholics. Reverting to early Childhood memories, I can still remember before my Siblings and I being sent to bed we all knelt down to say a decade of the Rosary. I, not knowing the importance of Mum and Dad's devotion of this `ritual`, I would sit on my Dad's back as he was kneeling down and kid-on I was on a Horse and calling out, "Hi-ho, Silver, away" imagining that I was `The Lone Ranger` off the TV.   Show. They soon put a stop to that.

Chapter 2

My early days at school?   I was a skinny wee freckled-faced boy who the `Bullies` thought was a soft target. How wrong they were.

   The `Bullies` (or uneducated sons of uneducated parents to me), were no more than cowards who covered their limited intelligence and personality with their size and ugliness.

For example, their was one bully who loved me too bits (for the book we will call him Baw-bag) Baw-bag always wanted to hang out with me because he thought I was a funny guy. He always laughed at my patter and jokes but I was not to tell the other `bullies` or he would `kick Fuck out of me`.

I asked him often why he didn't want the other Neanderthals to know about our friendship and he said... (And to this day, I do not understand why...) *"If they knew I was hanging about with `one of the wee-er guys` I'd get my head kicked in".* (Baw-bag, what a shit-bag)

Baw-bag, (real name, Johnny) however, was deep down not really a bad lad. He just felt he had to keep up this persona because he was big and ugly enough to fit into the category of `bully`. He stayed a few `closes` down from me in Craigielea Drive. Anytime he came up to my door to see if I was going out to `play`, my Mum wouldn't let him in the house. My Lovely Irish Mother could tell a nice person from an ass-hole. (God Bless you Mammy) His older brother, Billy, joined the Army and was killed when he stepped on a mine. (I do not think he wanted to do that!) There was nothing left of him to bury. How devastating was that for his Mammy and Daddy? To lose a son (in whatever manner) and to be left with `Johnny`?

I met Johnny in the High street in Paisley some many years after School days and he introduced me to his new Wife. I said *"Hi, nice to meet you"* but I had to hold my Laugh in. Not that she was not a nice looking Woman or Ugly. The humour I found was that,, because Johnny was not a very good `Bully` he had , some years before, lost his two front teeth in a fight and his new wife , who he was very proud of (and why not ?) had the `biggest` `buck-teeth` I had ever seen. My immediate thought was, *"Aye, You fit in together".* My thought however, never left my mouth. Anyway, I still think of Johnny as my friend, and his Brother,

God rest you Billy. And possibly God rest Johnny, (I think that he is now with his brother and his long gone Mum and Dad)

Yes! School days. `The best days of your life? ` Maybe for some, but for others, it must have been absolute Hell.

Not for me, I loved them as I had

so many friends, both bullies and wee shit-bags. For whatever reason, I got on with everybody. I think, with the bullies, they could not work out why I wasn't afraid of them and always answered them back. (I got a few `slaps` off them but I never lowered myself to run away or cry) They dubbed me *"the boy who wouldn't cry"*. As for the `wee shit-bags`, I think they liked me for much the same reason. I used to love showing how much braver I was than the so-called `hard- men.` When I got `the belt`, I never drew my hands away. When the `hard-men` were about to get the belt I would say to some class-mates to count out loud how many times the big coward drew his hands away…..`Whoosh !!` *"One"*, `whoosh!` *"Two"* and so on. This also made the Teacher go mad so, when he did make contact, it was a mightier `wallop` than it would have been if Mr hard-man was hard enough not to avoid the `whooshes` and take it like a man in the first place. (Shit-bag)

Alas, most of the guys I knew at school, I lost contact with after school years were over and we had all been `educated`. I am sometimes reminded of certain schoolmates by people who ask me *"Do you remember `so`n`so?"* and, although the name is familiar, I can't put a face to it. Other times I've had people say to me *"Hi Neilly"* (or Con, as I was also known) and I know the face so well but, I don't know their name. Some people, however, stay in your mind. Two guys I knew from secondary school for example, were the Markie twins. (Was it markie?) I think one was called Gerry and his twin brother was called Martin. Gerry was the funnier of the two but martin was funny in his own way. He was the `less intelligent` twin who just acted the clown (intentionally or naturally, I've never been sure) He was clever in some ways like, if he and Gerry wanted to go home, Martin could `vomit at will` and was allowed to go home with his brother as an escort. Brilliant! It never failed.

Another guy who sticks in my mind was called Ian Motram (who was inadvertently responsible for me learning how to play guitar… Why?? I will explain later on). Ian stayed in Renfrew and myself in Ferguslie Park. We had, one year, both by coincidence, got a scalextric set for our Christmas. We had this great idea to put both sets together so we had a bigger racetrack. So, we would go to one and others houses on alternate Fridays after school.

The Markie twins and Ian were not from my neck of the woods. They were schoolmates but, some schoolmates were from `Feegie` (Ferguslie Park). Big Peter Crawford, Eddie O`Conner, Joe Rush, Peter Rush, Billy McTavish, John (Jethro) McDaid, Jake McMulkin and Denis McBride, to name but a few.

However, I shall tell you about most of these guys later.

MY FAMILY
Chapter 3

I have never been a book reader. I always seemed to be too busy, or be the type who, `waited for the video to come out`. Not that I have not read the odd book before. To me, it just seemed to take up too much of my time. I have however been reading a couple of books recently and they have given me a sort of guidance as to how a book should be written.

Apart from the `introductions` and `acknowledgments`, (that I now realize are put in place once the `story` has been written) I have discovered that you have to go back to the `beginning`.

So, I shall try and not `jump` ahead of myself and tell you about something that belongs later in my story. (Like I have done already!)

Meanwhile, I must mention my first day at School. (Before I met the `Bullies` and `wee Mammies-boys` who were to become my class-mates)

I can remember my Lovely wee Mother taking me there on my first day. I can remember sitting at the table drawing a `BIG MONSTER` on a piece of `back-to-front` old bit of wall-paper when Mammy said, (in her Lovely Irish accent)"*c`mon now `neilis... we can`t be late fir school*". "*Can I just colour in this bit of Blood that's coming out the Monsters eye Mammy??*" (Even at that age I had an unhealthy, morbid fascination about scary Monsters and Ghosts. .Weird? I know) "*No!! B`jacus! ....., ye can finish it later*" Mum shouted, as she grabbed my hand and led me to this unknown place of intrigue, fear, wonder and amusement.

Indeed, I had this morbid fascination of all things Ghostly and Supernatural. I do not know how or why I had it, and from such a young age? It was cause for concern for a time for my Mum and Dad as , (thanks to inheriting the talent for drawing from my Dad) I always drew MONSTERS, GHOSTS, SKULLS and, for whatever reason, people (mainly cowboys) hanging from a tree. I would use, as a canvas, the reverse side of some old wallpaper and draw or paint a life-size `DRACULA` or `FRANKENSTEIN` or   `THE WEREWOLF` and hang them on my bedroom wall. This obsession however, was not to follow me in my later years, (apart from still loving horror movies and loving my early working years working as a nurse in the old `Mental` Hospital, Riccartsbar in

Paisley).
Little did I know that through my life I would meet some people who were so dispicable and downright monstrous that they would make THE WERWOLF seem like a domestic pussy.

I will disclose the identities of these horrible people later. They shall be named and shamed.

MY FIRST LOVE (I THINK)

Chapter 4

`IN AND OUT THE DUSTING BLUE-BELLES... (Repeat twice more) I AM YOUR MASTER`.

was the song we used to sing during this Play-ground game where everyone used to stand `arms-around-shoulders` in a big circle and (going clock-wise) the `Master`, after weaving in and out of   the circle, would `tip-a-rip-a-rappa` on your shoulder making you the leader of the ever-growing snake to weave `in-and-out` the aforementioned Blue-Belles. Usually, you would get `tip-a-rip-arappa`d` by your friend. So, when Katie Porter (a beautiful blonde class-mate for whom I had an inexplicable attraction to,   being only 7 years old) Tip-a-rip-a-rappa`d on my shoulders, I was so excited and thought "Yeah, she likes me" So, eager to please (and show-off to my new-found, and first female friend), I proceeded to intertwine the blue-belles with a bit of a `swagger` knowing that my `babe` was right behind me hanging on to my shoulders…………but, I suddenly realized that I was swaggering on my own with no hands on my shoulders. *"Why are they still singing?? Where`s my new Girl-friend?? What`s happened??………."*"SHIT!!! Why did I go anti-clock-wise???"*…My first ever experience of embarrassment and a game I never ever played again telling the teacher *"That`s a rubbish game"*

Katie, as I remember, emigrated to Australia the year after. (Yeah! that`s what I thought…she took it bad.)

I was to `fancy` a few of my female class-mates at Primary school. Not knowing why I `fancied` them. I obviously knew nothing about sex or `winching` (snogging) or the birds and the bees. I just knew that I liked the look, the smell, the long hair, and the legs and (even at that age) some of the Girls had a curious couple of wee `swellings` on their chest. I also had this strange comfort when I was having a bath and washing myself down below. I was 7 years old but I think I must have had `past life memories`. How else can it be explained? 7 years old?????

One Girl I remember

was called May Monaghan. I was told, (long after I had gone to the boys-only secondary school), that she used to `fancy` me. If it was true or not, I will never know but, after thinking about it, I wish I had known as she was a really good looking Girl.

I remember one day I was `cleaning` the `black-board` at the end of lessons and May was to lock-up the class-room. She said to me *"Neil, are you going to be long as I have got to shut this door in a minute"* I meant to say to her that it`s o.k., *"close it. I`ll lock it."* But, what came out was *"SHUT IT!!"* She never spoke to me again.   If ever you get to read this story May, I`m sorry.

I have actually said hello to May a few times in the past few years when sometimes, shopping at the local `ASDA`, and, having the `Should I? Will I? Ask her if she remembers that day feeling, and then say "Sorry"? Then I think, "NAH!"

Chapter 5

My Wonderful, Beautiful Mother was from Gurranebrather in Cork City. One of the 5 Children of Daniel and Kathleen O'Brien. Mum was (I think) the 4th born after Chris, Bridgette and Mary, and Lizzie being the youngest. They were all raised at 246, Cathedral Road, where my Aunt Lizzie still resides to this day. My Wonderful and funny Father was born in Paisley. He was the son of Thomas and Mary O'Gormley. (The only Grandparent I ever knew was my Granny Mary who passed away when I was 11 years old)

My Mum and Dad never spoke much about their past, even when asked by myself and some siblings. Their reasons why are now with them in their shared Grave at St. Conval`s R.C. Cemetary in Paisley.

I only got smitherings of their past lives like, Mum`s Dad was a bit of a rascal who had `allegedly` `stabbed` his first wife during some sort of stupid argument and then fled to London. (She was o.k. and not killed as a `stabbing` would suggest) There are no official records or reliable verifications of the incident so we cannot condemn Granddad. It could have been an accident, a miss-understanding, or maybe he was an evil Bastard?? We will never know. My Lovely wee Mother however, never believing that her Daddy could do such a thing, wanted to find where her Daddy was buried. Somehow, Mum and Aunt Lizzie decided to do their `COLUMBO` and made enquiries to some London based relatives as to where their `outcast` Daddy lay. They, seemingly, were given some clues from the, *"It wasn`t me that told you"* relatives as to where Daddy would be found…They indeed found their Daddy`s unmarked grave and `adorned` it with a Crucifix, a bunch of Flowers and a Prayer. He can now rest peacefully where he is in his, (thanks to his Lovely Daughters), newfound Grave.

My Dad was a Paisley man whose Family were obviously Irish. I don`t know why, but my Dad wanted to go to Ireland (maybe because his `step-brothers`, Joe and Paddy still resided there) He decided, when he was about 16  or 17 years old, to `run-away` from Scotland and head across the Irish Sea in the hope of meeting up with his `Irish` family.   For whatever reason, he ended up in Dublin. Having no money or anywhere to stay he ended up `busking` by playing the `Penny Whistle`. I do not know where he obtained this musical talent from or indeed who taught him but, seemingly my Granddad (Daddy's Dad) was a musician of sorts.

Dad never did, at that harrowing time, ever get to meet up with his step-siblings. Instead he was becoming a `Gentleman of the street`. A nice way of saying a Hobo, a Tramp, and basically a `beggar`. But, my Daddy was a beggar with a Talent. He survived by playing `rebel song tunes` like `Sean south `, `Green fields of France`, `Black velvet band` `When you were sweet 16`…(which are not exactly `rebel songs`)

Being the Man he was, he decided that he was not a Hobo, not a Tramp. And not a busker. (And he needed a bath) He was better than this. So, what did he do?? Go back to Scotland to his Mammy (who he missed so very much), Try and find his step-siblings?? NO` He joined the Irish Army. (Not the I.R.A.)

I remember having a drink with my Lovely Dad and him telling me that the only reason he `joined-up` was because he was `starving`,` cold` ` not very good at busking` and `really` needed a bath. He must have been very good at the busking as he made £5.00 in one day………..in 1936?? How much is that worth now??

I can remember my Dad`s sense of humour. It was basic and obvious, but still original. Sometimes I think that he did not know how funny he was. It was not like my Mum`s `un-intended comedy` (and she was funny). His humour was just so natural. I remember when I was about 11 or 12 years old watching him having a shave. I was mesmerized with all this `white foam` he was scraping off of his chin and neck. He said to me. .*"No` be long until you are doing this son…    What age are you now?? 11? 12? Anyway,"* (he was about to give me my first lesson on shaving) *"Always remember, after you have shaved to take out the blade and rinse & dry it. Otherwise it will get rusty, and you don`t want to be shaving wi` a rusty blade"* He was `un-screwing` the old-type razor to take out and clean his blade when he noticed that he had two blades in the razor. With him looking somewhat bemused at the two blades, he said to me *"…Now, if I* *had known that there were two blades in there I would have cut myself"*. To me, that was so funny but to my Dad, it was just another funny observation. He couldn`t help himself. He was just a naturally funny guy. Two of my best Friends, Denis McBride and Jake McMulkin were from the same `school` of natural wit. More about these guys later.

My Dad`s Sister was the Lovely Cathy. She was married to Jimmy Docherty and they had 4 Children, Brendon, Kieran, Angela and Kathleen. They resided in Barrhead (a suburb of Glasgow but regarded as a part of Paisley …where, indeed the aforementioned resting place of my Parents, St Convals Cemetery is situated). Aunt Cathy was My Dad`s younger sister. They were both the Children of my Wee Granny Mary, my Granddad's second wife. Hence why Dad went to Ireland to find his Step-Brothers.

I don`t know much more of the Family

history at this point but, if I can remember or get told any `snippets` during my time writing this, I will add them later.

One of Mum`s classic comedy moments happened one day when I arrived home and Mum was in the Kitchen getting Dinner ready. My Dad was due in from work about 3 o'clock so I asked Mum if she needed any help in preparing dinner. *"Not at all Son, I`m fine"* she answered, so I went back to the living room with a cup of tea and sat down to do the `Daily Record` crossword. As I sat there I could hear Mum humming away to some old Irish tune as she prepared the dinner. Then I heard this noise, *`B`DOINK`…B`DOINK` ……. `B`DOINK …`B`DOINK`. "What the hell is that?"* I wondered. I went through to the Kitchen and saw Mum `bouncing` this mug off the concrete floor and catching it. *"What you doing Mum?"* I asked. *"I bought dis in town when I was out earlier"* she said. *"Dae say it`s an un-breakable mug, look…"*

`B`DOINK`. *"Oim goona get one for ye as well"* *"Oh that`s good. Dad will like that"* I told her and went back to doing my crossword.

After a few more `B`DOINKS` Dad got home. He settled down with his book awaiting Mum to say Dinner was ready. *"What you making for Dinner Norah"?* He called, *"Oi got a lovely piece of Haddock today and oim making Chips and* peas *with it"* Mum replied. *"Oh that will be lovely"* Dad said.

I then went through to pour the tea when Mum asked me to call on Dad.

"Dad, Mum wants you for a minute" I called. Dad came through to the kitchen still with book in hand and looking over his glasses, *"Aye, what is it "?* He asked as he looked at Mum with the `un-breakable` mug in hand slightly raised above her shoulder. *"Watch dis Conny"* She let the mug drop to the floor… SMASH!!!!

The `un-breakable` mug was in tiny pieces

on the kitchen floor. Mum had a completely baffled look on her face and Dad just looked at her, looked at the broken mug on the floor, looked at me then looked at Mum again. *"Aye. Very good Norah"* he said, looked at me with an inquisitive look on his face and returned to the living room and his book. Me?? I was doubled over laughing.

Chapter 6

—

`THE BOY THAT WOULDN`T CRY`! Yes, that is what they called me during schooldays. Also `THE BOY THAT DOESN`T SWEAR`. Swearing? It was a natural language for these people who I went to school with. It was part of their vernacular. It certainly was not part of mine. I was brought up by knowing that `bad-language` was not acceptable in any situation. You just did not use swear words.   For years I did not know what to call my (now that I know it's proper name as `Penis`), my wee pee-thing. I was not to call it a `wullie` or a `johnny` as they were `swear` words. (This was way before we all now know it as a `prick`.) Cornered by 3 or 4 `bullies` in the toilets at primary school, who I would not give my `dinner-money` to, they would say things like *"You're the wee hard-man that'll no cry or swear `in`t yi?"* *"Aye, that's me, so what?"* I would retort (again, not showing my fear). *"Oh Aye???? Yi think yi`r a wee hard man?? If you don`t say `FUCK` or `CUNT` or `BASTARD` or "leave me alone," "Ah`m gonni punch yi`"*

Still, with the belief that my Mum and Dad had taught me that these people were just Cowards and trying to justify their very cowardly existence,
I would deny these ass-holes the pleasure of making me adhere to their wishes of making me cry or swear. Yes! They could punch me, (but they very

rarely did). Eventually, they would end up saying things like *"You`re no shit-bag wee man. Hey! you`re ma`h wee mate.""* anybody gives you any shit, let us know". "Aye, right, o.k." I would reply, as the `big ugly shit-bags left to try and constitute their existence by `pulling -up` another wee skinny freckled faced guy. Little did these Bastards know was that I was indeed scared and did not want to be `punched` in the stomach (which is very, very sore) That, once they left and I was on my own, I cried and I swore…I cried with Pride that they did not get to me, however scared I was, and that I swore that they would never even think about `pulling` me up again…….."BASTARDS".

I`m getting older now. I can`t   remember at this point of my story until just about starting `secondary` school..   St Mirrens` Academy, Renfrew Road, Paisley.

To cut a very log story short, I will start with my early thoughts of going to secondary school.

St Aelreds. A brand new built school in Glenburn, Paisley.

After being at St Mirrens Academy for 6 months, myself and 5 others in my class were told that we did not need to go to this new school, St Aelreds, as we had the academic qualities to stay on at St Mirrens and obtain some qualifications as in   `O` levels , `A` levels and some stuff even `higher`

I, however, thought that I would rather go to the new school along with my friends. Myself and 2 others declined the offer of `better teachings` and decided to leave St Mirrens. ..Bad move, I ended up doing what I`ve been doing since leaving school (with no qualifications) doing this job and that job. My other 2 friends ended up jobless and alcoholic. (Both dead now) The other three??? one`s a Dentist, one`s a Marine Biologist and the other?? An alcoholic (but, a clever one!)

It was at secondary school that I developed a `liking` for acting after the class was shown, (unusually for school) a `Movie`. The Movie was the great story of OLIVER TWIST. I watched. Feeling very envious of the young actors, as they were about the same age as me. *"I can do that"* I thought. Since then I was in just about every play or panto the school put on.

My English teacher, Mr Burns, thought that if I attended drama school I might just be good at it, so he enrolled me into the Citizens Theatre Drama School in Glasgow. This however was to happen in my 3rd year.

Meanwhile, back at 2nd year, I found myself hanging around after school wondering where my aforementioned Friend (Ian Motram) was. Like any other Friday, we used to meet outside the P.E. hall and proceed to one or others house to join our `Scalextric` sets together. I was also found `hanging around` by the `Janny`.

"Oi!! What you doing in here?? Did you not know the `home-time bell` has gone or are you deaf??"

After explaining about my missing friend he suggested that I try the Music room, *"They plinkety-plonk on their Guitars in there on a Friday"*.

Off I went to Mr Millers Music room and indeed, as I got closer, I heard what sounded like `plinkety-plonk type noises`.

I peered through the window of the classroom door to see if I could see my fellow `racing driver` but all I could see were all these kids sitting with Guitars that seemed more like a double-bass on their laps. Most of them were studiously looking at what I assumed to be Mr Miller or possibly the blackboard.

Some of them were `strumming` in a rather robotic style while others sat with there, `strumming hand` hovering just above the strings, eagerly awaiting their cue to join in.

I spotted Ian in this section of `Guitarists` and tried to attract his gaze away from the blackboard to the widow I was peering through. I only succeeded in attracting the attention of Mr Miller whose face appeared two inches away from me on the other side of the window. *"Ah-Ha!!, Mr O'Gormley I presume. To what do we owe the pleasure of your company??"* He asked sarcastically, after `swooshing` the door open and grabbing me by the collar.

After explaining that I was looking for my Friend, he told me to sit on my back-side and not to interrupt the lesson. *"We will be finished soon"* he informed me.

While I sat there on the aforementioned back-side, I watched with interest at the method he was using to incorporate the `not-so-good` strummers with the ¬not-much-better` ones. Seemingly, the `not-sos` only knew one chord and the `not-muchers` knew three.    The middle row had `in-betweenys` that knew 2 chords.

 Mr Miller was an excellent musician but could not sing a note. He would be on Piano `singing`, *Michael row the boat ashore, Halle-----""C major"""-----Lu ja----- """G major""",* instructing the strummers what chords to play. The ones who only knew one chord could obviously just come in when the one they knew was `instructed`. The middle row came in with their two chords, and the `smart-asses played all the way through the `vocally-challenged` rendition of the old religious ditty. I, meanwhile, noticed that illustrations of the Chords had been drawn on the `Black-board`. I could not work out why the ones who only knew one or two chords didn`t look at the illustrations and strum all the way through along with the `smart-asses`. *"Why don`t you play C major or D major??* I asked one of the one-chorders. *"I only know how to* *play G major"*, was his reply. A tad bemused by this, I pointed to the illustrations on the Black-board and said to him, *"The `D` & `C` chords are up there….see??) "Aye"* he said," *but it takes ages to learn them".* Thinking he may just be a wee bit slow in trying to understand the concept of the blatantly obvious illustrations, I asked to borrow his Guitar. After a few glances between the board and Guitar, I mastered the seemingly `difficult` chord of `C` major. *"See? That didn`t take ages to work out, did it?"* He looked at me in disbelief and said *"Aye right! Somebody has shown you how to do that before"* "Naw they haven't!!* I replied, quite loudly and a tad annoyed. That`s when Mr Millar intervened and asked me. ...sorry, told me, to wait outside as I was disrupting the lesson. I was just going to go home but Mr Miller told me to wait until the lesson was finished as he wanted a word with me. *"Aw Naw!!"* I thought, *"I`m going to get the belt"*

I stood outside the Music room for about 20 minutes before the budding `Hank Marvins` left the class. *"Mr O'Gormley!!!"* Boomed the beckoning voice of my executioner, *"In here NOW!!!"* I entered the class prepared to face my punishment with my usual determined attitude not to withdraw from the downward , 100 mile an hour, hard leathered, three tongued giver of pain, (but still wanted to run away). *"Have a seat, I want to ask you something"* said Mr Miller. *"Have you ever played a Guitar before?"* I sat somewhat bemused and surprised at the question, but, still looking out for the aforementioned `giver of pain`. *"No, Sir"*, I replied. *"Then how did you know how to play C major?? …"It`s up there on the Black-board"* I replied. *"You picked up a Guitar, looked at that illustration and played the chord??"* *"Aye Sir…sorry, Sir, Yes Sir"*. He looked at me somewhat suspiciously and handed me a Guitar. *"O.K. then, plays the D* *major and the G major"*. Starting to believe that this `detention` was not going to be one of painful palms, I asked *"Which chord first Sir??"*… *"D major"* he commanded, as he sat there on his desk, crossed legged, Thumb on chin, and index finger stroking his unkempt Moustache. *"D major? o.k. … just have a look! Right that finger goes there, and… o.k. .. . This one here and, Got it! Ring finger…eh! Here? Right…. `STRUM`."* I looked at the now very inquisitive tutor of all things musical waiting, hopefully for any sign of approval. *"G major"* he demanded, still stroking his un-trimmed facial hair. *"O.k. this one looks easier. That finger there…that one? o.k.! …and, erm. m.m, right! That one there."* …STRUM. Feeling quite proud of myself, I awaited for a response from Mr Miller. *"You have learned that by looking at the illustrations on the Black-board today, and you have never been shown how to play a Guitar before???"* *"Yes Sir, is that good??"* I asked, hoping that it would save me from the three tongued monster. *"Well, Mr O'Gormley, if you are telling me the truth then I honestly think that you have a natural musical talent".* He told me that, `the experts`, a.k.a .the `smart-asses`, who knew the three chords, had taken him months to teach how to do what I had just accomplished in the short time I was there.. I was quite surprised to hear this but, I was more surprised as to how long it took them to learn, what I was later to know as, ` simple chord `shapes`. Not really knowing what to say I nervously smiled and said, *"What!? Are they daft??"* I don`t think it was the right thing to say as, Mr Miller, it turned out , was very proud of what he had achieved thus-far with his Guitar class students. *"How dare you presume that my pupils are not capable of learning how to play a musical instrument!! It does not mean that they are Daft, as you so delicately put it Mr O"* He boomed. *"Sorry Sir, I didn`t mean to………………..",*

"QUIET, BE QUIET!!" he boomed even louder. By this time I was rubbing my hands preparing for what I thought I had originally been summoned for (and for thinking that I had been a smart-ass) *"Sorry Sir. Can I go home now ? I only ended up here looking for my pal. I`m supposed to be going to his house tonight to"*…….

"Quiet!!!" he shouted again with his intimidating, deep but tune-less baritone voice. *"Here`s what I want you to do".* Folding my arms again, (well ! actually hiding my hands from the `belt`) I said " *What`s that Sir ?".* He sat and looked through his briefcase and eventually pulled out some sheets of paper that had the `chord-shapes` that had been drawn on the Blackboard and handed them to me. *"Take these home with you. You will notice that there are more complicated chords illustrated. I want to see how quickly you can learn them. Take them home and practice and I will see you after school*

tomorrow" *"I will do that Sir, but I don`t have a Guitar".* **He then went to a small cupboard at the end of the class and took out a Guitar that was still in it`s Guitar case and said,** *"Here!,* *" This is my Guitar. I can`t let you take any of the schools instruments".* *"Thank you sir, but I can`t take it home with me"* *"And why the Hell not ??"* **He `Boomed` ..**" *Because I`ve got my `scalextric` with me and I can`t carry them both home."*

I, of course, left my Scalextric` in the safe keeping of Mr. Millar who stored it safely in the aforementioned cupboard where his Guitar had been tucked away.
A few days later when I was supposed to bring his Guitar back, my Mum kept me off School because of a `sore tummy`,
I got a Friend of mine to take the Guitar back to Mr. Miller for me.
`BAD IDEA`. When I returned to school the

following day I went to see Mr. Miller with intentions of impressing him with my quick learning skills on Guitar.

"Have a seat Mr. O" He ordered. He then took his Guitar from it`s    flimsy plastic case. *"And what happened to my Guitar ??"* he asked, holding it from it`s broken fret board.

It had snapped in two and I tried to explain that it was fine when I gave it to my Friend. I was thinking the worst, The Belt, Having to pay for the damage or at least a kick on the Arse, but he soon put my mind to rest and told me that my `friend` had been on his way to the classroom to deliver the Guitar when he slipped and fell on top of the poor unfortunate stringed instrument. He then let me show-off my `talents` on another more fortunate guitar and praised me for having `a natural talent`.

He said he would give me further lessons. I was looking forward to it, but about a month later he left the teaching to join a

Folk Band.

I thought, *"Awe, Folk sake"*.

I did however learn to play eventually by teaching myself.

LEAVING SCHOOL
<u>Chapter 7</u>

The end of the first 6 month of 3rd year and myself, Howard Cairney, Brian Dock, Eddie O`Connor and Ian Mottram are told that we have the intellectual ability to stay on at St Mirrins Academy and possibly acquire O level or A level qualifications if we stay at St Mirins and not move to the `New School` in Glenburn . (The aforementioned St Aelreds).

This meant, instead of being in class 3A, we would then be in class 2B for the next 6 months. I thought *"going back a year and down a grade ?? Naw !!*

I would rather go to this new school in Glenburn with my many (dumb) friends and leave school at 15 . Looking back, I was the dumb one.

On leaving school I went from one job to another. My first job was in *Aitkins Dairy* loading and unloading Milk floats with crates of Milk. I was getting paid £3. 10 Shillings (£3.50p), not too bad in 1968 but my `dig-money` was £4.00 a week.

I left that job and was employed in other places like `*The Woolgrowers*` in Brown st. (A place that many years later would the scene of a very sad episode in my life.) `*Carlton`s dye casting*` in Stock st. `*Stoddards Carpet factory*` in Elderslie, `*John Temple the tailor*` on the High st and one or two others before I got to being a `Student Nurse` at *Riccartsbar Hospital`..* Now there was a job !!

Studying psychiatric patients and realising that the Human Brain can be one `Fucked-up` organ at times.

These guys were on a different planet.
Senile Dementia, Schizophrenia, Bi-polar,
Dissociative Disorder (*Multiple personality disorder*) Korsakoff`s syndrome….. And that was just one guy !!
(o.k., it wasn't)

I had been studying Nursing   there for a couple of years when I gave it up to take a job as Hospital Porter…in the same Hospital.

The reason for this `strange` decision was that the Porters job was more money than the Nursing. I was 19 years old and had two Daughters and one on the way. I married a girl called Mary Murphy who had moved to Ferguslie Park with her Mum, Mary, Brothers, Peter and Frank and step Dad Tam Mackin. Her Mum and Tam then had a Son and called him David.

Mary was a bit of a `head-turner` and we hit it off almost right away.

We had been seeing one and other for just

over a year when Mary fell pregnant. We had in fact split up before we knew of the pregnancy and were still not together when our baby was born.

Mary refused to tell her Mum who the Father was and was blaming it on a guy who travelled with `the shows`. The minute her Mum set eyes on our Daughter she said, *"That`s Neilly O`Gormley`s wean" "She`s his double"*

Mary admitted that I was `Dad` as looking at the baby there was no question that she was mine. (Beautiful wee thing)

We eventually got together again and decided that to get married was best for our Daughter, (but not necessarily for us as it turned out)

Chapter 8

Our Daughter   was born on the 22nd of June 1972 and `adopted` by Mary`s Mum, also called Mary. They gave her the name

Tracy Mackin. That name was soon changed after we got married on 23rd November 1972. She was then Christened Theresa Marie   O`Gormley. On December 21st 1973 our second Daughter Lynn was born and then our third Daughter Connie Blessed us with her arrival on March 20th 1976.

I was a very proud Dad   of three Beautiful Girls. I never knew you could Love as strong as the Love I still have for my Daughters.

Eventually myself and Mary split up. It was sad in a way as the first 4 or 5 years Mary was a good Mother and Wife. I however was a good Dad, but a terrible husband. I thought nothing of `one night stands` with other women. I believed that if I done so it did not mean that I did not love my Wife. Very stupid and immature of me. That was the downfall of our marriage, that and the fact that Mary eventually realized that she didn`t really love me.

I had been seeing a young Nurse called Paula before and after the Marriage ended. We got on well and ended up getting a wee flat together. One night when we went to the pub after work she said she had some exciting news for me. *"Exciting news ? Have you win the pools ?"* I asked somewhat nervously. *"No, get the drinks in and I`ll tell you"* she answered. I went to the bar to order the drink and was dreading what she was wanting to tell me. I returned to the table and sat down beside her. Then she took my hand and with a loving look in her eye she looked into my eyes and said, *"I`m pregnant".* I was stunned. *"How can that be ? You`re on the pill aren`t you ?"* I asked. She said that she wanted to surprise me and thought it would secure our relationship. *"Secure our relationship ? I got three Daughters with my ex wife and that didn`t secure that relationship".*

I explained that, although having a baby is

a wonderful thing, this was bad timing and she should have discussed this with me before coming off the pill. *"I`ve got three Daughters and my youngest is only two years old, I have still to work out what I am going to do with my life after being divorced and the last thing I need is for you to tell me you are expecting our child".* As much as I liked Paula there was never ever going to be a lasting relationship. Talk about putting a spanner in the works.

We split up not long after that night, but Paula wasn`t long in getting another man in her life. She called me at work one night asking what time I got off. *"I finish at Nine, why ?"* I asked. She said she wanted me to meet her new boyfriend Tony as he wanted to ask me something. I met with them both in the pub and introduced myself to Tony. He was a lovely guy and you could see that he was in love with Paula. He went on to say that he and Paula were getting married and he wanted to let me know that he would be bringing up my child as his. I thought that this would be for the best considering the circumstances and knowing that my child would be taken care of.

I shook his hand and promised that I would not interfere in the upbringing of my child, but stressed that if in the future the child wanted to find out who their real Father was, I would welcome the child with open arms. As the night went on I asked Tony what his surname was. *"Lawler"* he said, *"Tony Lawler"*. That`s when I nearly choked on my pint with laughter. *"What`s so funny ?"* he asked. I turned to Paula and said, *"Do you realize what your married name is going to be ?... Paula Lawler"*.

Paula gave birth to a lovely Daughter who she called Ashleigh. For years I wondered what she was like and if she looked like any of my other Daughters. I even told my three Daughters that they had a younger Sister and that hopefully the could meet some day. 34 years later I get an email from Ashleigh asking if I were her biological Dad. She said that she had heard my name mentioned many times when she was growing up and she noticed that I was also on her Mum and Dad`s friends list on Facebook. I wrote back immediately and told her I was her Dad and was so happy that she contacted me. I told her that she had three big Sisters, Four Nephews and three Nieces. She was over the moon and we arranged to meet.

I emailed Paula to tell her the great news but was shocked and surprised by her reply. She wrote back saying, *"You had no bloody right telling her you are her Dad…I told her who her Dad was and that he died four years ago. Just keep your nose out of my Family`s business".* Somewhat taken aback I answered. *"What you talking about ? I`m her Dad. Either that or you have lied to me for 34 years, not to mention cheating on me back then.. What about Tony telling me he was bringing up MY Daughter while you were sitting there ???"* I was shocked, but did not believe her. She also never got back to me.

I went ahead and invited Ashleigh up to my place where she met my oldest Daughter and, as we believed, her older Sister who was up from Bournemouth on a visit. She looked very like my other Daughters and her and Theresa hit it off right away. We discussed what her Mother had said and Ashleigh told me that she was indeed told that her `real` Dad had died. I told her about the night I met her   Dad (Tony) and that as far as he knew, I was her Dad. She said she asked him about that and he said that her Mum admitted after about 11 years that I was not her real Dad. My Daughter Theresa could not believe that Paula would let me believe that Ashleigh was mine for all these years and said she would pay for a D.N.A. test.

About a week later the D.N.A. test kit arrived and we sent off the samples right away. The results were due back in one week but I had booked a holiday in Turkey for that week. Ashleigh said she would pick me up at the Airport on my return and hopefully have the results of the test with her. The reason for me going to Turkey on my own was what could only be explained as a sentimental journey. I will explain the sentiments later.

I returned on the Friday and sure enough there was the Lovely Ashleigh to pick me up. We sat in her car and she read out the results to me. With a tear in her eye she told me that I was NOT her Father.

To this day I still keep in touch with her as do my three Daughters. I still believe that she is my Daughter. I still find it incredibly inhuman and evil that a woman can allow a man to believe he had a Daughter for all those years. I`ve heard many a time that these D.N.A. kits purchased from internet companies are often wrong. It was suggested that I should call the `Jeremy Kyle` t.v. show but`, I have nice Teeth and wouldn't have got on.

Chapter 9

At the time of Ashleigh's birth I was still working as a Porter at the Royal Alexandra Infirmary in Paisley but, this was soon to end not long after Ashleigh was Born.

It was a Sunday evening and I was supposed to be on the Nightshift with two colleagues, Bobby Killoran and Big Hughie. Before starting our shift we were in The `local` bar, (The Wellington) where they were holding a Charity Night and the three of us were there to help with the `fundraising` before going to do our nightshift. Hugh however had a wee bit too much too drink and decided to `phone-in sick`... as did Bobby Killoran. Knowing that it would be no problem to get the shifts covered I then decided that I would do the same. I called my Dad and asked him to `phone-in sick` on my behalf. Dad told me it was a bad idea but, phoned in anyway. Once he had done that I then had a few `pints`.

Not long after the `Boss` came into the bar and told myself and Bobby that our shifts had been covered o.k. (Hugh had left by this time) So we carried on and enjoyed the rest of the evening… even getting invited up to the Boss`s house for more beers. All was fine and jolly until a few days later when myself and Bobby got a letter from head office requesting a meeting with the `Boss`s `Boss`s`. The Boss had reported us for being at the pub after phoning in sick !!

We got seen individually with our Union rep, Brian McCorkindale present. Somehow, Bobby got off with it due to a `technicality` but, I was shown the door. Brian advised me to appeal the decision through `Disparity of treatment` (Both Bobby & me were accused of the same misdemeanour but, I got sacked and Bobby didn't)

I got the necessary form to fill in and when I did so I gave it to porter John Laird who was the `mailman`. I waited and waited for an answer to find out when I would have my `hearing`. I told the union rep Brian that I had not heard from anyone regarding my appeal for over two months. Brian checked it out and was told that they never received any letter of appeal and it was now too late to request one.

John Laird (the mailman) was a close Friend of the Boss.

You do the maths.

The Boss by the way was a chap called Bill Gellatly.

He was a likeable rogue, a bit of a Ladies man and was reasonably fair with myself and my fellow Porters, well! Until he got me fired.

I loved my time working at the Royal Alexandra Infirmary in Paisley. I had many a laugh and many other `perks` like Nurses, Radiographers, Domestic cleaners and other Females from different Hospital departments.

But, despite the lovely `perks` what I remember most is the Laughs.

One of the great `pass-times` on the nightshift (after the usual mayhem had calmed down) was phoning random numbers in the middle of the night. We had three phones in reception that we could `hook-up` to each other. I would call a random number and get some poor sod out of bed while my shift-mate was doing the same on another of the phones.

Once we got an answer we would say *"Hello. This is the international operator. I have a call for you from Australia. Do you wish me to put it through?"* once they answered, *"eh… aye, o.k."* I would ask them to hold the line while I put the call through. Once my shift-mate had successfully got through to his `victim` and said the same we would then say *"O.k., Thanks for holding. Putting you through now"*.

We would listen in and piss ourselves laughing at the confused conversation of our two `victims`. (victim 1)*"Aye! Hello. Who's that?"*…. (victim 2*) "This is Andy. Who are you?"* (victim 1) *"I'm Willie McCardle. Who are you and why are you calling me at this time of the Morning?" (v1) Ah never called yi, you called me!) (v2) "Naw a didney. You called me! An` ah don't know anybody in Australia")…* Sometimes it turned into a real funny argument and other times they got on well with one and other. It was way before you could call 1471 to see what number had called you. Apart from prank calls and general funny things that happened day in and day out, there were some scary events too. One Nightshift on a very Stormy night. . . `Stormy night sets the scene for a scary story`….. Myself and shift mate, John Verlaque, settled down in reception after a very busy evening of casualties (mainly drunks) RTAs (Road Traffic Accidents) and various other unfortunate incidents that required Hospital treatment. We had let our older shift mate, (Auld Tam, aka Uncle Snifter) go home about 01.am as he had been on a double shift.

Myself and John settled down with a pot of Tea and some `Jaffa Cakes` and, as it was a stormy night we started telling one and other Ghost stories

The weather outside was like what you would see in a `Hammer House of Horror movie` so we were hoping that we didn`t get a call from any of the wards to remove a `body` to the Mortuary. John was telling a story of one night he was walking home from the pub and had this feeling that he was being followed. He kept looking behind him to try and allay his fear. He never saw anyone but, just had the strongest feeling that there was someone or something following him.

Just then I said to John, *" Shush!!! What's that noise??"*

"What noise?" John replied. *"Listen. . . Can you hear that?"*, I repeated. *"Oh shit!! What the fuck is that?"*. What we could hear was a sort of `gurgling` noise like someone choking plus what sounded like `staggered` footsteps. We only had the night lights on so anyone the other side of the reception desk the light was behind them and you could only see a silhouetet of them until you switched on the desk light. Suddenly the `Silhouette` appeared before us. It was a Woman who had entered by the side door and slit her throat while approaching reception. The Blood was spouting from her wound. Covered in Blood (as were me and John) we got her on a trolley and quickly took her to the A&E. Alas, the poor lady didn`t make it. She died in Theatre.
"What was the outcome of John`s spooky story?" I hear you ask. Well, as I said he had the very strong feeling of being followed and kept checking behind him but, saw nobody, UNTIL. . . (imagine the

dramatic music at   this point in your mind). . He got to his door and while putting his key in the lock he turned and saw a very tall dark `figure` at the edge of the path leading to his front door just staring at him. John ran in the house and locked the door. He then went to the window to see if the mysterious `dark figure` was still there. It had gone!!!! More `spooky` stories (and funny ones) to follow.

Chapter 10

While   working at the Hospital I had other `casual` relationships with Nurses, Radiographers *(they could see right through me)* Receptionists and Cleaners. I was a proper Dog.
One of the relationships was with a Beautiful looking Student Nurse called Lynne Cosh. I thought the World of her. She was also a funny and Intelligent girl.

We stayed together for a while in a flat in Causeyside st.

I was with Lynne for about a year and a half before we broke up.

We had mostly a good relationship but, like any other, we had our ups and downs. At the time we were together I was playing in a band called `The Mill Street Blues`. Myself and Three Policemen. (Mill St is where the Police office is in Paisley, hence the band name). The Keyboard and Accordion player was my good Friend, Joe Cairns. Joe was actually better at playing accordion than Keyboards. I used to say to him at times when he was finding difficulty playing any part of a tune on Keyboard, *"Turn it on its side, Joe. Imagine it's an Accordion"*.

We once got a booking for a Wedding in Newcastle which was fine but, Joe's then Girlfriend (another Lynne) was a tad upset as the gig in Newcastle was the day after their Wedding. We done the gig anyway. After the gig myself and Lynne spent the night in a lovely B&B as did big Ian the Drummer and also a guest singer. Can't remember her name. I think it was, Tracy. Because of some mix-up in booking the B&Bs, Joe and his `brand-new` Wife had to spend the night sleeping on an old single `Army` bed in part of an old Army barracks. She wasn't too pleased.

It was in May that year (1981) that I lost my job in the R.A.I. and also broke up with Lynne.

I was back staying with Mum and Dad and was a tad lost as I had never been unemployed before. I had a bit of Money left over from my time working in the R.A.I. and doing the odd gig so I was able to go out most nights for a Pint or Three. After a few Months of looking for a job and going out for Pints I was out one night and visited the Wellington Bar where most of my Friends from the Hospital frequented. From there I headed for another bar called `The Tea Gardens` hoping that maybe one or two of my Musician Friends would be in there doing a gig.

Sure enough there was my old Friend, Henry singing his wee Heart out. I ordered a Pint and stood at the bar enjoying the singing and atmosphere when some girl called out, *"Neil furra song"*. I turned to see about 6 Girls sitting at the corner table. I vaguely recognized one or two of them from attending some of my gigs in `The Crown Bar` in the west end of Town. They asked me to join them so, thinking it would be rude not to. I did. *"When you back in `the Crown singing?"* asked one of them. I told her I would be there on the Saturday.

"That's good, we will be there. It's my Sister, Donna that wanted to know. She fair Fancies you."

I looked at Donna and remembered seeing her once before. I remembered her Beautiful smile and her lovely Eyes.

Just then, Henry asked me to go up for a song. I asked Donna if there was any song she would like to hear and she said, *"Could you sing that Dr Hook song, `Carry me Carrie`? I heard you sing it in the Crown and I've loved it ever since"*. I said, *"of course"*. I then went up and taking the Guitar off Henry I said, *"This is dedicated to the prettiest Girl in the room. Donna"*. Little did I know that night that I would spend the next 30 years with that Lady with the Beautiful Smile and Lovely Eyes.

Chapter 11

Before I tell you about my 30 years with my Beautiful Soul-mate and Love of my life, Donna, I feel I should return to my teenage years as I have not mentioned some great Friends I had at that time.
School friends like Peter Crawford, Eddie O'Connor, Brian Dock,   Rab Elliot, David Mannion, Harry Tunstead, Howard Cairney, Joe and Peter Rush, John (Jethro)

McDaid, his Brother, Jimmy McDaid, Billy McTavish. Denis McBride and Jake McMulkin. Not all in my class in secondary school and others who were not at the same school. Other Friends were Billy and Pat Hampson, Twins John and Duncan Lamond and others too many to mention. I have not met many of them since Schooldays but, because of modern technology like Facebook and Friends reunited, I have been able to catch up with some of them.

I caught up with old School friend, David Mannion a few years ago on Facebook. I remember one day back at School in Art class, David was picked out to be `the Artist's model`. He sat posed on a chair on top of a desk. The Art Teacher was quite impressed with my drawing of the aforementioned model saying that I had really captured his `pose` and it was a good likeness to the `subject`. I'm just glad that David wasn't posing as a nude model.

More recently I saw picture of David on facebook wearing a T-Shirt with print on it showing support for Scottish Independence. I asked where he had purchased it as, (although I now reside in Bournemouth) I was all for an Independent Scotland instead of such a potentially great Nation being dictated to from Westminster.

David then told me that he printed said T-Shirt himself. He told me that printing `Personalised` T-Shirts was a side-line of his. I got interested in this `side-line` and he told me how to go about printing and selling them. I have been doing so ever since. Thanks David.

Out of the Friends listed above I know that, Denis McBride and John (Jethro) McDaid have unfortunately passed away. (r,i.p. Lads)

I had known Denis since the age of Five. My Parents and Denis` parents were very close as they all came over from Ireland about the same time (circa 1948) and settled in

Paisley. Denis and his Parents lived in Logan Drive and we lived in the next street, Craigielea Drive.

Although I also knew Denis from School, we hung about more when my Family moved to Crawfurd Drive in 1968. (just after I left School.) We stayed in number 5 and the McMulkins stayed in the next building. I was good Friends with Jake and Hugh McMulkin. Jake's best Friend was Denis. The 3 of us ended up being great Friends and socialised for years, each one of us as funny as the other.

Denis and Jake were both great, and talented guys. Jake was a good Guitarist and singer/songwriter but, never ever wanted to join a band and strut his talents on stage.

Denis turned out to be a brilliant Guitarist. He had decided to go for `Classical` Guitar lessons when he was 15-years-old which paid off soon after when he was wanted by a lot of Paisley and Glasgow bands as their lead guitarist.

I played alongside Denis in a couple of bands, namely, `The Peter Dute band` and `Spot the Dog`. The other two members of `Spot the Dog` were Bass player Jim McKechnie and Drummer, Willie Watson. Two great guys.

Willie the Drummer was quite a small guy who was affectionately known as `Wee Willie` but, whenever Denis spoke to him he would refer to him as `Wee Willie, (nothing personal) Watson.`

My good Friend, Denis lost his Life to Cancer in 2008 and John (Jethro) McDaid some years before. R.I.P. Friends.

Another of my aforementioned Friends, Billy McTavish I will be forever grateful to. My ex-Wife and I were separated for the first time after about 4 years of Marriage and one day I got a call from her saying some lowlife had tried to `snatch` our Daughters, Theresa and Connie. Theresa would have been about 8-years old and

Connie about 4-years old.   They had been to Mass at St Fergus` with a couple of Theresa's older Friends but, got separated on the way out. As they stood outside waiting on their Friends, some weirdo approached them and grabbed their hands saying, *"Come with me, I know your Daddy and he's waiting for you"*. Theresa told him that Daddy was working and was coming down to see us later. The weirdo gripped her hand tighter as she tried to get her and her wee Sister away from him. He told them just to walk with him and not to scream or he would hurt them. He forced them from outside the Chapel on Blackstone Rd, up King St and along Main Rd to the Ferguslie Park. Once there, he was trying to put them over a wall where they would not have been seen by anyone in the Park. Just then Theresa saw `Daddy's pal`, Billy McTavish. She called out to him, *"Uncle Billy, Uncle Billy, help"*. Billy recognized my Girls and started to run towards them The weirdo let them go and ran as fast as he could. Billy was determined to catch up with the lowlife but, stopped to comfort the Girls and take them home to Mum. It was lucky for the Bastard lowlife because, if Billy had got a hold of him he would have killed him. My Girls are now in their early 40s and still remember that awful day. I'm forever grateful to Billy for deciding to go for a Pint in the Park Bar that day. I dread to think what would have happened to my Baby Girls if he hadn't.

DONNA LOVE.

Chapter 12

The most Beautiful Eyes, the most Beautiful Smile, a gentle Loving nature. The first Three things I saw in the Lady I was to spend half my life with.

After singing Donnas request, `Carry me Carrie` in the `Tea Gardens Tavern` that night in 1981, I rejoined Donna and her Friends at the corner table, I took a bow and donned my imaginary Hat to Donna then kissing the back of her Hand I said, *"For you Sweet Princess"*. Donna just laughed but, her Sister, Rita said, *"Check oot Sir Galahad there"*. I replied with, *"The Days of Chivalry have not yet gone when in the presence of such a vision as Donna"* Followed by, *"And now Sister of this Vision, ah`ll have a Lager"*. I Sat with Donna and Friends for about a half hour when her Friend, Nancy said, *"That's the Taxi outside. Donna, you'll need tae get a Taxi wi Sir Galahad as the Driver can only take Five"*. *"Quite a subtle set-up"*, said Donna. I said *"Suits me. I will see you home if you would like"*. When Donna said she would like that, I felt this strange sort of `warmth` inside me.

Little did I know that I, the 28-year-old Sir Galahad, would be with this Beautiful Fair Maiden until I was a 58-year-old.

At the time of meeting Donna I was back staying with Mum and Dad and Donna stayed with her two Sons, Stephen and John in Sutherland Street. We were both divorced by this time. After `dating` Donna for a few weeks I moved into her house and got on great with her Sons. Her younger Son, John was football-daft and loved St Mirren.

Ex St Mirren Captain, Jackie Copland had just bought the Pub where I was a regular, `The Crown Bar` in Paisley's West-end. I was telling Jackie all about wee John's obsession with St Mirren when Jackie suggested that I should get Donna to bring him into the Pub to meet him. I phoned Donna and told her what Jackie had said and to bring wee John to the Pub.

Donna said, *"Oh my God, he'll be over the Moon to meet* one *of his Heroes"*. Donna called on wee John and told him that I wanted him to meet one of my Friends up at the Pub. She never told him who the

`Friend` was. After about an hour Donna and the wee man turned up and I said to him, *"Hi, John. I got someone through here* (the lounge) *who wants to* meet you". *"Who is it?"*, he asked, *"I don't know anybody that goes to the Pub apart from you and my Mam"*

"Never mind that." I told him, *"He knows you".*

He walked through and saw Jackie standing there. *"Hi, John. How you doing, mate?"* said Jackie while offering John a handshake. His wee Face lit up on realizing who was standing there. *"You're J…J…Jackie Copland!!!!"* Jackie said, *"I know. And you're J…J…John Brines".* Jackie then gave him a Cola and a bag of Crisps. *"I've got some stuff for you, wee Man".* said Jackie then presented him with a Football, a St Mirren book and various other St Mirren memorabilia. Donna, who had a wee tear in her Eye said, *"Awe, look at his wee face"*

We stood at the Bar and let the wee Man discuss football matters with his Hero. He was over the Moon.

Before we left Jackie told us that he was going to get wee John a job as a Ball-boy at Love Street. When we got home John couldn't wait to tell all his wee pals. They were all out playing football in the street when John ran up to them and started dancing around and singing, *"Ah know Jackie Copland, Ah know Jackie Copland, Ahm gonny be a Ball-boy, ahm gonny be a Ball-boy"*.

The next day Donna told me that John was walking home from School with one of his school friends. They were walking past `the Crown` on the other side of the street and John had been telling his wee Friend that he was Friends with Jackie Copland. *"Naw yi urny`"* said his wee pal. *"Aye ah um"* said John. Just then Jackie pulled up outside the Pub in his flashy Red Volvo. Getting out of the car he saw John and called to him, *"Awe* right John?" . *"Aye, no` bad Jackie, mate"*, answered John as he carried on walking with a bit of a `swagger`.

I had been with Donna for about a year and a half at this time and we were enjoying our lives together but, tragedy was about to strike.

About a week after Wee John had met his Hero, Jackie Copland, I was at home waiting for Donna to come home from work as a Home-help. She would call me and ask me to peel the Potatoes for either Chips or Mash. I was happily sitting peeling the totties when Wee John came up from the street and asked what was for Dinner. I told him that I wasn`t sure but, your Mum asked me to make chips for tonight and I didn`t know what we were having with them. I said to him to go back out and carry on kicking his new St Mirren ball about with his Friends. *"Okay", I'll look out for Mum coming home, See ya".*

About 20 Minutes later Donna got home

and said, *"I saw John out there playing football with his Friends and told him I would give him a shout when Dinner was ready. I just need to sit down for 5 minutes with a cuppa before I put dinner on".*

I got up and made her a wee cuppa. She had hardly taken a sip of it when one of John's friends came to the door. *"Mrs Brines, Mrs Brines. Johns fell!!!. Mah Mammy's phoned an Ambulance".*

When we heard the word, `Ambulance` we thought he's probably broken an Arm or a Leg but, it was much, much worse.

While having a `kick-a-bout` one of his Friends had kicked the Ball up onto the roof of a warehouse   belonging to the `Woolgrowers`. None of John's friends wanted to climb on the roof to get it so, as it was John's special Ball, he decided to climb up and get it himself. While he was gingerly making his way along the roof he stood on the Perspex skylight and it gave way leaving the wee Man falling through, hitting his

Head on one of the Steel girders and landing on the Concrete floor about 50 feet below.

Donna and I went in the Ambulance with him. While in the Ambulance he started to go into a type of fit but, the Ambulance attendant managed to calm him down. The Attendant was a Friend of mine that I knew from working in the Hospital. His name was Raymond'

Once we got to the Hospital I pulled Raymond aside and asked him how bad the Wee Man was. He told me it was really bad. The `fit` he had in the Ambulance he actually

Died but, Raymond managed to get his Heart pumping again.

After about an hour the Doctor took me and Donna into the A&E office and told us that her Son's Skull had been shattered and splinters of it penetrated his Brain. There was absolutely no chance of survival. It was only the `Machine` that was keeping him

alive. I put my Arms around Donna but, she was completely numb. The Doctor then said, *"I know this will be so difficult for you to answer at this moment but, time is of the essence. Will you allow us to use your Boy's Organs so as others may live?"*
Donna looked at me with the tears running over a slight Smile then looked at the Doctor and asked, *"Does that mean that my wee Boy's Eyes will see again and his Heart beat again?"* The Doctor told her he would not only give someone the gift of Sight but, probably the gift of Life to maybe 5 others. At this point I saw the strength of this Wonderful Lady when she told the Doctor, *"Take what you need if it means my Son is still alive in some way"*. What a Brave, Brave Woman. Apart from her Beautiful Eyes, her Beautiful Smile, I now saw the Beautiful Soul. Is it any wonder why I Loved her so much?
Wee John lost his young life one week after his 11th Birthday and on the traumatic day

of his Funeral it was such a Beautiful Sunny day. Hundreds of People, Family, his Friends, and Parents of his Friends, (and Jackie Copland) were there to say goodbye to this Child and I could see the Heartache in everyone's Eyes. Wee John was (and still is) Loved by everyone. A lovely wee Child who Loved his Life and his Football like most 11-year-olds do.

My feelings were for Donna. I was thinking to myself *"How is Donna going to get through this? How does a Parent handle the loss of their Child?"* It must be the most horrible thing for a Parent to suffer.

At the Wee Man's Funeral, Donnas Brothers, Drummond and Hughy, were Pall-bearers along with myself. Donna and I went home shortly after and we just sat, had a wee drink and Cuddled. I told her how proud I was of her as to the way she was so strong about how she had handled the whole situation then she looked at me with her tear-filled Eyes, kissed me and held me tight, then Cried her Heart out.

I also Cried my Heart out.

We decided a few days after that we should get away for a few days and Donna arranged that we would go down to Maidenhead to spend some time at her Sister, Maureene`s house. We got the Coach down on the Thursday, a week after the Wee Man's Funeral. On the Saturday we went through to Bournemouth to visit my Daughters. My Girls were so upset as they had met John and got on great with him, and his Brother, Stephen. They were young and couldn't understand how or why this had happened.

Donna was lovely to them and tried to tell them that, sometimes, these things happen and then told them, *"Wee John is happy and in a good place. Don't worry about him. He is an Angel now".*

I can remember my Girls asking Donna to go and put her Swimming costume on so as they could all go for a wee swim. We were at the Beach after all.

Donna said, *"okay"* and then went to the `changing area` to get her swimming gear on. (did I mention that Donna was the West of Scotland Schoolgirl Champion at one time?)

Anyway, when Donna left to go and change, my Daughters started to cry and hugged me and said, "Daddy, please don't die". They had experienced for the first time that someone the knew had passed away.

After a nice day with my Daughters we headed back to Maidenhead.

We got back and Maureen had got a few beers for me and a couple of Bottles of Wine for herself and Donna.

Donna noticed that her Sister was upset and told her "It's *okay Maureen. My Boy is in a better place although I wish he was still here with me"*

"It's not that Donna." Maureen said. *"I have got more bad news for you"*. Donna asked her, *"What can possibly be worse bad news*

than me losing my Son?" Maureen then told her that earlier on when we had been in Bournemouth that their Brother, Drummond had been run over by a Bus in New Street and killed.

Her wee Boy and her big Brother gone within a week?

How was Donna going to handle this?

Chapter 13

LIFE GOES ON.

Most of you will have at sometime in your life lost a Loved one. A Parent or both, a Sibling, an Aunt or Uncle, Cousin, Nephew, Niece or Friend.   All Heartbreakingly sorrowful but, to lose a Child must be the worst Heartache of all. Check the Thesaurus for any other description of the word `Heartache` and it wont offer one word to describe how you would feel. Like Donna, my Lovely Irish Mother lost a Son. My older Brother, Daniel in 1996. He was

45 and lost his life to that most evil of Satan`s Serpents, Cancer. Only 5 years after my Father by the hand of the same `Serpent`.

My younger Brother, Paddy also lost his Son in 20th March 2006, aged 18. More recently, my younger Brother, Chris lost his Son, Stephen to a Brain Haemorrhage in 2017.

As they say, "Life goes on". After Donna lost wee John I was reluctant to leave her side wanting to make sure she was coping. I cancelled `gigs` that I thought were too far away and after a while I just done more local ones while making sure that someone was with Donna. This went on for a few Months until Donna told me that I should not worry about her and that she would be fine. I told her that I thought it was still too soon to leave her but, she said, *"I miss by Boy but, I still have Stephen and you."* I humbly agreed but, it did not stop me worrying about her, not for a while but, as time went on, I once again saw the strength this Lady had within her.

It was now time to try and carry on with life without wee John. Donna started going out again with her Sister, Rita and her best Friend, Nancy. They loved going to `Paddy's Market` in Glasgow every Thursday. (don't know what was so special about a Thursday) and now and again they would spend a weekend in Blackpool or get on the Ferry to Rothesay.

One Friday they had there bags packed and were just about to make their way out the door for a `Rothesay` weekend. I gave Donna a kiss and told them to enjoy themselves. Just then, the phone rang. I answered it and found myself speaking to a `Radio Clyde` DJ called `Emperor Rossco`. (Can't remember his real name) He told me that he was looking for solo or double musical acts that could do the remainder of the Summer season in Santa Ponca, Mallorca and would I be interested. He said that flights, meals and accommodation would all be included as well as a weekly salary.

I said, *"Yes. When do I leave?"*. *"Tomorrow, if it's not too short notice for you"* he answered. *"Does my Wife get for free also?"* I asked while looking at Donna`s inquisitive looking face and still holding her Suitcase for Rothesay"

He told me that my Wife would of coarse be included in the deal and she could either travel with me tomorrow or anytime in the 6/7 weeks I would be out there. I obviously said thank you and to tell the people I would be working for to meet me at the Airport in Palma once I find out the time of the first flight out there.

I looked over at the door and Donna and co were still standing there and still with the inquisitive look. *"You 3 still here? You not got a Taxi waiting outside?"*. *"Never mind the Taxi. I heard the words, Mallorca, free flight and* accommodation. *Who was that on the phone?"* She asked.

I said, *"Well. Put it this way. I've got a gig or 2 for the next 6 or 7 weeks over in Spain. You can come with me tomorrow or go to Rothesay for the weekend and fly over and meet me there on Monday"* You're winding me up." She said. *"I bet that's either Paddy, Denis or Jake on the phone."* I eventually convinced her it was not a wind up and she would be having a free 6 or 7 week holiday in Sunny Mallorca.

I managed to get a flight the next day but, Donna couldn't make it out until the following week as she had to get time off her work as a Home help and also get someone to keep an Eye out for her Son, Stephen. I phoned her after about 5 days and it was Stephen that answered. *"Hi Stephen. Is your Mum there?"* I asked. *"She's down at the shop. She should be back in about 5, maybe 10 minutes".* I said, *"O.k., I'll call back"* . *"Hold on Neil. You wouldn't have heard about Rachel".* Rachel was the Girlfriend of my good Friend, Denis McBride. She was a Beautiful, Funny and Kind Girl who thought the World of, not only Denis but, also my 3 Daughters. *"What's happened? Is she o.k.?"* I asked him nervously. He then told me that she had taken an overdose of some type of prescription pills and killed herself. I was in total shock and could not understand why such a sweet person would do that. I remember thinking that you never know the pain people go through when they can hide it so well, and don't show it so as not to upset the ones they Love for fear of upsetting them. While I was having a great time working in Spain and so much looking forward to Donna coming over, this news brought me back to reality. After thinking about this terrible news I thought, After what Donna had to go through and now this. Life, indeed must go on.

Chapter 13

Before we settled for a new Life in Mallorca, Donna and I had been a typical couple getting on with life the best we could. Donna had her job as a Home-help and I was `Plucking my G string` and singing in the Pubs, Clubs and Hotels. I was never one for going on Holiday as I thought, if I'm on Holiday, I'm not out earning money. It was the same when I worked at the Royal Alexandra Infirmary before I had even met Donna. One time I was told by `the Boss` that I had to use up my remaining 2 weeks Holiday time before April or I would lose it. I took a week off and visited Bournemouth to visit my Girls but, that was fine. I not only got time off work but, I got a couple of gigs while I was there and made more money than I would have earned in one week than at my job in the Hospital. (there's no business like show business.) I still had one week to take when I came up with a `cunning plan`. I knew one of my shift mates had used up his Holidays and would dearly love to have at least another week in England to visit his Son who was working at some Golf course. (Don't remember where exactly) I suggested to him that I would sell him my remaining weeks Holiday to him. *"Is that even possible and if so, is it legal?"* he asked. I told him that I would put in for my time off but, instead of him coming to work, I would come in and do his dayshift and clock-in and out with his time-card. We checked it out with the boss and he said, *"As long as you clock-in and clock-out, I'm not bothered who is doing the shift. And keep me out of it if it goes `Tits-up`"*.   We agreed that I would do his weeks work under his name and he paid me a weeks wages plus, I had my Holiday pay on top of that. What could go wrong??

Not a lot we thought but, although I was always on time to start my, Early shift, Back shift or Night shift, I was never on time for a Day shift. Unfortunately, my work mate returned from his unofficial

Holiday and received a `Verbal warning` about his tardy timekeeping. `He` was late every day for a week. He hunted me down and when he caught up with me he was livid. *"Ah got a verbal warning about my time-keeping for last week and I've never been late for work in my Life!!!"* He rather angrily shouted to me. Trying to hold my laugh in I said, *"What's that got to do with me? I was on Holiday last week"*. He never spoke to me again for ages.

Anyway, Donna eventually convinced me to `try out` Spain. We ended up in a Town called Calpe, about 15/20 Miles North of Benidorm. I had asked Donna while we were there not to say to anyone that I was an Entertainer as I thought it would be nice to listen to someone else doing the same job as I did for a change. We had arrived late on the first night so we sat in the apartment and had a wee drink. Donna went to bed about midnight and I went downstairs to the Hotel bar. While at the Bar I got talking to an English couple who said that they had been coming to Calpe for a few years. I asked them if there was any decent `live music` acts in town and they said, *"You need to go to `Dave's Bar`. There is a guy who sings and plays Guitar every night. He's from Belgium and he is the best you will hear in the Costa"*. I was tempted to tell them that I also sang and played Guitar for a living but, after me asking Donna not to reveal that to anyone we met, and the fact that this Belgian guy was maybe better than me, I decided not to. The next morning I suggested that we go and see this guy later in the Evening so we met up with the couple I had met the night before and they took us to `Dave's Bar`. We had been there for about a half hour and got introduced to the Bar owner, Dave. There was a guy sitting playing Guitar and singing who, basically, was shit. Donna asked `Dave` when the guy from Belgium , (the best in the Costa) was coming on. Dave said, *"That's him"*.

I had been away furry pee at this time and when I got back Donna said to me, *"Get up there and give them a song"* I said that I would rather wait until the Belgian guy had been on to see how good he was. *"That is the F###in` Belgian guy, noo, get up and gie them a song"* She insisted. She then asked `Dave`, *"Can mah man go up furra song?"* Dave said he would go and ask `the best in the Costa` if that would be okay. He came back and said, *"Sure he can. I told him it's Neil?".* After about two awful sounding songs later the `best in the Costa` called on me to come up and give a song. I went over and took his cheap Guitar off him and noticing that there were quite a few Irish holidaymakers present, I decided to sing, `*When you were Sweet 16*`. It went down very well and I got the biggest cheer of the night. I was asked to stay up for another song or two, so I did. It would have been rude not to. I gave the `cheap Guitar` back to `the best in the Costa` and he carried on with his show but, it was quite embarrassing as people were shouting, *"We want Neil, We want Neil"* while the guy was trying to sing. I would have died if that happened to me. Poor guy. Before we left the `best in the Costa` called me over and said, *"You didn't use a Plectrum,* (Guitar pick) " I said, *"No. I was `finger-picking`"*. *"Can you teach me how to finger-pick?"* I said, *"Sorry mate. I'm only here for a week."* The next day at our Hotel we were sitting by the pool when the Hotel Manager approached us and said, *"I heard from a few guests who were at Dave's Bar last night that you sing and play Guitar. I have a band here at the Hotel tonight and was hoping that you would sing some songs for us. You and your lovely lady can have free drinks if you do."* You can guess my reply. The band that night had set-up by the Pool and, as promised, I got up and done about a half hour gig. Being Spain, it was such a Beautiful evening and singing outdoors was

a new and pleasant experience for me.
We never went back to `Dave's Bar` that week for obvious reasons but, I did go up for another few songs at our Hotel the night before we left. On the flight home Donna said, *"Well? Would you come back to Spain?"*. I said, *"In a Heartbeat. Thanks for convincing me to go"*. *"So much for you wanting to keep your job a secret"* she said with a sarcastic but, lovely Smile on her Beautiful face. She then told me that she was so proud of me. It was lovely to hear that.

We were not to experience Spain again until I got that phone call for Santa Ponca as Donna and co were Rothesay bound.

Chapter 14

Donna was more of a `House` drinker than me. I was a Pub drinker. I never liked sitting in the same Pub for any more than a

Pint or two so, when going out furra Pint I would leave our Sutherland Street flat and start off my `Pub crawl` at the West end, make my way East towards the High Street popping into `Jorries (formally the Bowlers Tavern), `The Wee Howff, `The Argyle Bar` and `The Bull inn`. Maybe have a Pint in `The Club Bar` then `The Court Bar` and eventually my last call, `The Elbow Room`. Normally you would have to go to most of these Bars to encounter a host of strange and funny Characters but, The Elbow Room had plenty of these Characters under the one roof. It was full of all sorts. It was a Family owned Pub owned by a nice guy called Eddie Murphy. It used to be a small Bar called, `The Sheep`s Heid` on the corner of St James` St. and Caledonia St. When Eddie took over and renamed it, The Elbow Room, he extended it to make a Lounge/Dancehall and called that part, `More Elbow Room`. It had entertainment every night of the week and opened till

01.am. When Donna wanted to join me in going out for a drink, we usually went there. It was only a 5 minute walk to get there and a 10 minute stagger to get back.

The place was full every night mainly due to the entertainment and late closing, and the fact that back in those days your Giro was worth more than what it is today.

I had a few gigs there at the time but, I had more when the Pub was taken over by a chap called, Isaac English.

I am still in touch with Isaac and also with Gary Reid and his Brother, Scott who both worked behind the bar. Many a night we had a few `Gibbering Juices` (Vodka & Coke)

I got Gary a job in Mallorca doing his DJ in my Friend, Pepe`s bar known as `The Oasis` and later he got the job as Karaoke presenter in `The Thistledome` which is now known as `McTavishes`, and later he worked in `The Jaggy Thistle`. Gary ended up staying there longer than I did.

Others I remember from the Elbow Room are, Terry Carling, Rab Prentice, Ronnie Piggott, Jimmy Rice, George Thorley, and a whole host of the lovely Lochrie Family. George Thorley played Drums and used to play alongside his Friend and Accordionist, Eddie Lochrie. Gary and I used to call them, `U2.` When Eddie asked why we called them that Gary said, *"Every time punters walk in here and see you an George on stage they say, Aw F##k !! no` you two again"*.

It seemed that every time mourners came back to the Elbow Room after a Funeral, `U2` would end up playing there even if they hadn't known the deceased.

Ronnie Piggott suggested that they probably looked in the `Paisley Daily Express` to see who had died and if it said that all are welcome back to `the Elbow Room`, George would call Eddie and say, *"Funeral mob at the Pub Tuesday. Grab your squeeze-box."*

Great days we had in the Elbow Room. Most nights some of the `regulars` used to stay after time for a lock-in. Sometimes it was `a lot ` of regulars. On one night after I had been playing there must have been at least 15/20 of us enjoying a drink and having a Laugh when we heard someone banging on the door. Isaac went to see who it was and discovered it was the Police. *"You are aware that you are breaking the Law by serving drinks at this hour"* said Mr Policeman. *"As far as I know, as long as I am not selling or taking money for the drinks and being the owner of the Bar I can have my Friends stay for a free drink"* said Isaac. *"So, these people are all your Friends?"* asked the aforementioned officer of the Law. *"Yes"* replied Isaac. *"Some of them are guests of `the band`.* The Policeman started to ask the regulars for their name and if they were Friends of the Bar owner or `with the band`. Just about all of them said, *"Ah`m wi the band".* They eventually got to me and asked who I was. I said, *"I am the band".* Both officers laughed and said to Isaac, *"We're with the band as well"* and ordered a couple of Whiskeys before leaving, without paying obviously.

Isaac was an ex Boxer who actually Boxed for Scotland but, I don't know in what competitions. His Son. Isaac played professional Football and played with Partick Thistle for a while. I can remember once he scored a fantastic goal against Rangers, (his Dad's preferred team) and I said to Isaac, *"If your boy comes in tonight I want to shake his hand".* Although his boy scored against his `preferred` team, Isaac told me he was so proud of his boy and, *"That Goal? Wow!"* Isaac junior did come to the Pub and his Dad told him that I wanted to shake his hand. Young Isaac asked me while shaking my hand, *"Is this because of the way I scored the Goal or because I scored it against Rangers?"* I said, *"Both".* As you can probably tell by now, I love the Glasgow Celtic but, I also Love St Mirren.

The stories I could tell you about `The Elbow Room` could be another book. (note to self… that's possible)

Owner, Isaac had his rather funny moments at times. One day he arrived at the Pub and noticed that the young Barman, John, was working behind the bar while the sole of one of his shoes was flapping about. Isaac said to him, *"What you doing coming to work with your Shoe flapping about like that? Could you not have worn better shoes to your work?"*. Young John said that these were the only shoes he had and would have to wait till he gets paid on Friday before he could buy a new pair. Isaac shook his head and then pulled out a wad of money from his back pocket. Young John's Eyes lit up. Isaac then pulled the elastic band from the bundle of notes then handed it to John. *"Here"* said Isaac. *"Wrap that around you shoe till Friday"*.

Chapter 15

The Medium

Donna always told me that she thought that maybe she had Psychic abilities as she swore that after her Mother passed away she saw, and spoke to her in a `Dream` but, Donna was sure that she was still awake. Some people call this experience, `a visit` and it has been documented all over the World from Millions of accounts as an actual event. Me, being a bit of a sceptic, suggested to Donna that it may have seemed real and because of the Grief you were going through and the loss you feel that, in a way, must be wishful thinking. Donna was adamant and said, *"Neil, I did see and speak to my Mother. I know that for a fact. I don't care how you or others analyse   it, I know it was real."*

I told Donna, *"If you believe it, then it is real"*.

She had other instances that enforced the feeling she maybe had that Medium or Spiritual instinct.

Her interest in the possibilities that there was a way to contact `the other side` was strengthened by a visit to a `Medium` in Glasgow who couldn't possibly have known anything about Donna. It was way before `Google` and the Internet era began. The Medium said to Donna, *"I have a Lady here. . I'm getting a name.. I think it may be your Mother or an Aunt and I'm getting the letter, `J` and she paid you a visit not long after she passed"* Donnas Mother was called, Jessie. Donna was obviously thinking, *"How the Hell can she know that?"* but, she was more convinced when the Medium said to her, *"You have someone who you are very close to, still living, who's initial is `N`"*. Donna never mentioned to her who that could be. It could be me (Neil) or her very close Friend, Nancy. Donna said, *"I have a couple of people in my life whose name starts with the letter, `N` and who I love very much."* Donna was taken aback when the Medium said, *"Neil. I'm getting the name, Neil"*. She then went on to ask if `Neil` had an unusual job. Donna said to her, *"You tell me"*, (thinking that this information was too accurate to believe) The Medium then told Donna that she didn't know what `Neil's` job was but, it wasn't a 9 to 5 job. She then asked Donna if she had ever stayed abroad and Donna told her that, apart from going on Holiday, she had never stayed in another Country. The Medium said, *"I can see you and the person I am sure is called Neil living somewhere Sunny and it's Neil's unusual job that will take you there."* About 5-years later we were living in Santa Ponca thanks to my `unusual` job. Myself and Donna spoke about this a few times when we would sit having a Beer, Wine, Tea or Coffee on our Balcony after I had finished my gig. Sitting there looking out across the Mediterranean, we often wondered if it were true that people could have `visits` from lost Loved ones and see into the future. Donna told me that the Medium she met in Glasgow didn't `look into the future`. She told her that her Mother told her that we would some day live in a Sunny climate.

Still wondering and interested in the whole subject of psychic phenomena, I remained mostly on the sceptical side of the subject. That was until the night my Much Loved Father passed away. March 31st I had just finished a gig in the Oasis Bar. Although it was still quite early for the Summer Season the bar had been very busy. I had only been back in Santa Ponsa for about a week after going back to Paisley to visit, and saying goodbye, to my dying Father. At twenty-passed 12 the pub phone rang and my Friend, Pepe, (the bar owner) answered and

then said to me, *"Neil. Tu* Hermano, Jose esta hablando por telefono". (Your Brother, Joe is on the phone)
I knew right away why he was calling me. Dad had passed away 5-minutes ago he told me. I was sitting at the bar Heartbroken and word spread among the `punters` who had enjoyed a good evening what had just happened. They were all so lovely giving me condolences and trying to find the words to comfort me but, as I said, I knew I had already seen my Dad for the last time the week before. Pepe poured me a drink and said, *"Lo siento mi amigo. Solo tienes un Padre"*. (Sorry my Friend. You have only one Dad)
About 10-minutes later Donna came into the Bar and just held me tight and said, *"I'm so sorry Neil. You know Dad* was *so proud of you."* We went home and sat on the Balcony and, not letting go of my hand, she let me go on and on about how Proud I was of my Dad.

It wasn't until the next day when I returned to the `Oasis that Pepe was asking how I was and that I didn't have to work that night. He then said to me, *"Who told Donna to come and get you last night? It was nice of them to do so"*. I said that I didn't know and I would ask her when I got back home. I was thinking that someone must have told her that my Dad had died, (there were no mobile phones or internet back then. We didn't even have a house phone.) I asked Donna how she knew to come get me and she said, *"Never mind. You won't believe me"*. I said, *"Please tell me as I would like to thank them"*. She said, *"Nobody. I woke up at quarter past eleven after having a dream about your Dad and just thought, I need to go and get you. I can't explain it"*

Dad died at 12-15am Spanish time. 11-15pm back home time.

Made me think, *"Did Donna see and speak to her Mother all those years ago? Did that Medium get told from Donna`s Mother that* *we would indeed live in a Sunny climate because of my `unusual` job? Did my Dad tell Donna that I needed her that night?"* I now believe that these things are True. Why do I now believe? Because, I got `a visit` from Donna a few months after she passed. I may have been in a `Dream-state` but, like Donna`s visit from her Mother, my visit from Donna was just as real.

You hear of things like this through your life and usually just ignore it or think, `It's all in the Mind`, `There are no such things as Ghosts`, `It's a load of Shit`, `If you're Dead then you're Dead` but, think you this before dismissing the possibilities.

What is it that makes you `be aware`? What is it that makes you `tick`? What is the power that makes you think? What is the power to make your Heart beat, to Breathe, to Function? Don't tell me it's your Brain as that also is another lump of meat like your Heart, your Lungs, and your Muscles.

Could it be your Soul? Then what is your

Soul?

Just like any electrical equipment you have, be it your T.V., Computer, Hi-Fi, iPhone, Tablet and so on. They are all `Dead` until they have electricity running through them. They are all useless, or `Dead`, until you `power` them up.

It's exactly the same with life. If the `Electricity` that powers you to function is not from a wall socket or battery, then it must be your Soul.

If your aforementioned electrical gadgets are broken, then they are broken but, the `Electricity` is still alive and kicking. When your Body is `broken` and can no longer function, what happens to your `electricity`, or Soul?

It is still an entity that `lives` on.

There is so much we do not understand about the World and our existence so, why do we question the possible existence of `Ghosts` and question the abilities of those who claim to see or to contact `the other side`?

I'm still not sure about `Mediums` as there are far too many Charlatans out there feeding off the Grief and wontedness of people who want to believe and, although these Grief-stricken people may be very intelligent and wary, they are also gullible at that time.

`Ghosts`, `Spirits`, whatever you want to call them are to me a great possibility. True or not, I have always been interested in the subject since I was a young boy. Especially since I remember one   time my Mum and Dad had some company at home. I think it was my Friend, Denis McBride's parents and the Parish Priest. I sneaked out of Bed and was hiding at the Living room door in the `lobby` listening to their conversation. I heard my Mum say that she had been in bed the night before and my young Sister was in the Pram at the side of the Bed. She said that she was awakened by `the Baby` crying and was just about to get out of Bed to go and comfort her but, before she got up, the Bedroom door opened. She said nobody was there and she heard the very quiet hum of someone `humming` the lullaby, Golden Slumbers. She woke up Dad and he also heard the `lullaby` and they both saw the Pram` gently rocking. The `Baby` drifted off back to sleep and Mum and Dad watched the Bedroom door slowly open and close again. Dad said to Mum, *"That was my Mother". She used to sing that Lullaby to me and my Sister, Cathy".* I was too scared to go back to Bed after hearing that but, Dad caught me sitting in the `Lobby` and told me to get back to Bed.

I knew that my Mother, being a devout Catholic would never lie and, especially not to a Priest.

When Mum came to visit myself and Donna in Santa Ponsa in the Summer of 1991 some Months after Dad had passed, I asked her about it. She told me that it was true and that I shouldn't have been listening to the conversation. Dad didn't tell her that I had been eavesdropping. She said, *"If I had known you were out of Bed and listening to us talking I would have kicked your Arse back into bed"*.

I know that most of you reading this Chapter do not believe in the Supernatural and I'm not trying to convert you. I'm merely telling you my story. Believe it or not.

Chapter 16

I've had many a Friend in my life and most of them
were, and still are, very funny and talented People.

They say, that growing old is a privilege that not all people are blessed with. As I get older I realise this to be true but, the downside is I have been to too many Funerals of my Funny and Talented Friends and, indeed Family.

As I mentioned earlier I was living in Spain when my Lovely Father passed away. I managed to get a Flight back to Scotland on the day of his Funeral but, unfortunately, not in time for it. I arrived back at Mum's house about 2 hours after my Dad had been laid to rest. Once I arrived my Uncle Christy, (Mum's older Brother) suggested that I and my 7 Brothers should drive up to his Grave and have a picture taken of `Dad's 8 Boys`. Uncle Christy said to Mum, *"I think that Conny would like that, Norah."* Mum agreed and said, *"That would be Lovely. I know he would Love all his Boys at the Graveside to say goodbye. And it be better that his Daughters stay with me."* Mum then handed us a `flagon` of Dad`s Guinness, (Dad's preferred libation) and told us, *"Once there each one of you take a sip and pour the rest on Dad's Grave.".* That's exactly what we did and each of us said, after taking our `sip` of Dad's Guinness, *"Goodbye Dad. See you in Heaven.",* (or sentiments similar) Uncle Christy then took a picture of us at the Graveside holding the Flower arrangement that spelled out, DAD. 5 Years later in 1996, Brother Danny passed away while living in Milton Keynes. All the Family traveled down for his Funeral which was another `packed-out` occasion. Danny was always a popular guy. He was always `the Ladies Man` and had quite a few relationships in his day. I remember my lovely Donna telling me that one of her Friends said to her not long after Donna and I got together, *"Donna. Are you going out with Neil O'Gormley?"* Donna said, *"Yes. I've been with Neil for about 8 months now. Why?"* Her Friend said, *"My first Boyfriend was his Brother, Danny. I really Loved him but, he chucked me for another Lassie. "Sounds like Danny"* said Donna. Danny had Married a Lovely wee Girl from Ferguslie called, June Johnson. They had 2 Children, Donna, and Daniel. They moved to Corby, (Little Scotland) as Danny had got a job in the Steele works, as many people from Scotland did back then. Unfortunately, like a lot of relationships, they split up and Danny moved to Milton Keynes as we had Cousins who lived there. Not too long after he moved, his Wife, June tragically   died and Danny took their Kids to live with him in Milton Keynes.

After some years he met and Married a Girl called, Carol and they had a Son called Neil. So, Danny's kids are called, Daniel, `Donna and Neil`.

Niece, Donna has a Daughter called, Connie. Also my Daughter's name.

Chapter 17   More sad goodbyes.

At the time my Brother Danny passed away I had been back from living in Spain for about 2 years. Donna and I were living in a nice wee flat in the South-side of Town in a street   called Mary Street. Although I was very sad about losing my Dad and, Brother

Danny within the space of 5 years I really felt for my Mum as I knew how she would be feeling after losing one of her Children as I had already saw Donna go through that unbearable Heartache. And so soon after losing her beloved Husband, my Dad.

When Mum's time came to be reunited with Dad and Danny, my Heart was, again Broken.

She had been suffering from Womb Cancer for a few Months and had been in and out of Hospital. The Doctors said that they couldn't operate as her Heart would be too week to come through such a procedure. How Ironic is the fact that the womb that had carried and bore her 13 Children would also be the Womb that ended her Life?

I always `popped` into Mum's on my way to work in the Hotels up the West Highland way. Mum was worried about me travelling these roads in the Snow or Rain. I would call in to see her and convince her that I would be fine and to see how she was feeling.

The last time I stopped off to visit I was on my way to the Loch Awe Hotel on Christmas Eve, 2009. She seemed okay and was joking about my Brother, Paddy's attempt to make her Dinner. I told her that I would get Donna down to make her Dinner and she said, *"No, no. Donna has enough to do taking care of you. Sure you're a worse cook than Paddy."*

I laughed and said, *"Need to go. I'll see you tomorrow"* Gave her a Kiss and left for my 1 and a half hour journey up North. I didn't know that about an hour after I had left that she was rushed into Hospital.

While she was in Hospital, the whole Family were up seeing her but, we had to take turns as there are so many of us.

Paddy, his Wife, Margaret and I said that we would do the `night-shift` and sit with her through the wee small hours every night. We did this every night for well over a week plus pop up through the day while our Sisters were doing the `Day-shift`. I remember when the Bells` chimed to welcome in the new year of 2010, I was holding mum's Hand and Paddy held her other.

Each day/night we watched her slowly getting weaker and weaker. She eventually went into a coma after about a week of being in Hospital and was comatose for about a week before passing. She would not let go. One of the older Nurses said that she probably doesn't want you to see her go. We thought that it was nice of this Nurse to say such a thing.

On the 10th of January while we all decided to go to the canteen for a cuppa and some of us for a Cigarette, Mum decided, `Now's the time`. My Brother, Paddy and my Niece, Fiona walked up to Mum's Bed just as she was taking her last Breath. We now know that the Nurse was correct in what she said. Mum did not want any of her Children to witness her demise. A True, Wonderful, Loving Mother till her last Breath.

It was suggested by some of my Siblings that I should write Mum's Eulogy to be read out at her Funeral by our oldest Brother, Joe. Apparently they decided that I should write it because, *"Neil has a way with words"*.

I considered it an honour to do so. I got to work on it and when finished I asked Donna to read through it and to give me her opinion. I printed it out and handed it to her with a wee cuppa. She settled down and started to read it but, only about 2 minutes of reading she handed it back to me saying she couldn't read anymore as it was too Heartbreaking. She then said to me, *"I don't think that Joe will be able to read this at the Funeral without breaking down. You should send it to him by email and let him decide"*.

I called Joe and told him what Donna had said about the Eulogy and I was about to email it to him. He said,

"Okay. I'll have a read and call you back"
About a half hour later he called and said,
"Donna was right. I am still in tears after reading it. I couldn't even read it out to *Rena,* (his Wife) *so what chance me reading it out in front of everyone at Mum's Funeral? Sorry Neil, you will have to read it".* Donna agreed with Joe as she said, *"You are used to standing up in front of a crowd with a Microphone."* I said, *"Yes, singing to them."* I did, however, end up reading it. And it was difficult doing so without breaking down. Donna was sitting with my 3 Daughters and they suggested that if I felt myself breaking down to look up at them to help me through it. I thought otherwise as, if I did look up at them, I would certainly have choked up. I walked up to the Pulpit and took a deep Breath and started to read.

"Today we say Goodbye to a very rare Woman.

A Woman who will be remembered for her Love of God,
The Love of her Family and, her Love of Life.
A Love that could be seen shining through her Beautiful Irish Eyes.

To look into those Eyes all that could be seen were Love, Compassion, Concern for others and, a cheeky wee Smile that proved that Irish Eyes do indeed Smile.
She was not the tallest Woman in the World but, as a Mother and Friend, she was a Giant.

I know she will be remembered with great Love and affection, not just by her Family but, also the many Friends who enjoyed her company.
Especially when they went on their Day trips in their wee Red `Postman Pat` van to Saltcoats or wherever for a wee Fish Tea.
Dressing up in various masks and wigs

leaving the locals to wonder what Planet they were from.

`So Good night Mum, it's time to rest, Dad waits for you above.
Through all your Life you guided us and showered us with Love.
We know that you'll watch over us along with Dad and Danny.
But, until the day we meet again, we will miss you,
Our wee Mammy`"

Donna had been suffering from a constant Cough for over a Month and was worried in case she would be Coughing throughout Mum's Funeral. She went to the Doctors a few days before to see if she could get some sort of Cough Medicine to prevent that from happening.
She was fine for over a Month being Cough-free until it returned in the February. She

returned to the Doctor who arranged for her to have an x-ray at the Hospital.

About a week after the x-ray she had an appointment to return for a Biopsy. By this time the Cough had gone and she was feeling fine however, a week after her Birthday on March 5th, another appointment was made for her to return to the Hospital for the results of her Biopsy.

The result was devastating.

The Doctor told her that she had inoperable Lung Cancer.

I had hardly any time to Grieve for Mum and now I had to prepare for losing the Love of my Life, Donna.

Donna and I were obviously taken aback by what the Doctor had just told us, *"Inoperable Lung Cancer???"* said Donna but in a calm and accepting manner. She seemed so calm about it and then turned to me and used one of my `catch-phrases`, saying, "*As you would say, Neil, Well. That was that*", and smiling when she said it.

We left the Hospital and while walking to the Car Donna stopped to light up a Cigarette. I said, *"Really??"* and Donna replied, *"Well, what's the point in stopping now?"*

We had both agreed that we didn't want the Doctor to give us a time scale of how long she had left in this World or as Donna said, "*Estimated Time of Arrival for Heaven, or wherever I'm bound for*"

Donna thought that if she was told maybe 6 Month or a Year that, as the time was getting closer, any ailment she got like the Cold, Headache or even the Toothache would make you think, `This is it`.

The Weird thing about the whole situation was that Donna felt well. She hadn't had the Cough for quite a while and she was full of energy. *"I've never felt better"*, she told her Son, Stephen.

She did feel fine up until she had her first

Chemotherapy treatment. A few days after her first treatment she had been feeling fine most of the day up until about 6 o'clock. She started feeling nauseous and also very weak. *"That's that F###in` Chemotherapy"* she said as I helped her to Bed.

She had been like this on and off for about a week or so.

She had said once that if ever she got Cancer she would refuse Chemo as most of the people she knew that had this horrible disease seemed to go `downhill` after the treatment. She said, *"Okay. It attacks and tries to destroy any Cancerous Tumours in whatever place you have it but, it can have a negative effect other perfectly healthy organs that have F##k all to do with it."* She had a way with words did Donna. I asked her why she wanted to go ahead with the treatment if she had been so against it, and she said, *"I always thought that I would be a good bit older than what I am now should I had got Cancer. I know it can kill anyone at any age.*

It doesn't give a toss but, I've always felt mostly healthy and now, I've got 2 Beautiful Grandchildren and another on the way, and I want to see them grow up. And, anyway, who's gonna take care of you? I'm not ready to go yet Neil."

On that first visit for her treatment she was still her usual calm self. Her name was called and we started to walk down the corridor to the treatment room. I was talking away to her trying to ease the worry I knew she was hiding and then noticed I was talking to myself. Donna had stopped walking and was standing some yards behind me. I approached her asking if she was okay. Then I noticed the tears running down her Beautiful face. The first time I saw her Cry since we first got the devastating news. Walking to that treatment room really hit home to her. That was the only time she openly showed how worried she had been. The other treatment visits she seemed fine but, she knew that I knew she wasn't.

After so many Chemo treatments the inevitable happened and she lost her Hair. She was fitted for 2 very nice and convincing Wigs. One day we arrived at the Hospital for what we were hoping would be the end of this session of Chemo, we were told that the treatment department were a little bit behind schedule and asked if we would mind coming back in about an hour. Donna said, *"Fine, no problem. I'm choking` furra Cuppa"*. I suggested we go to the canteen and `get a Cuppa` but, we first took a walk down to the Main entrance shop so I could buy a newspaper. We took a short-cut down a sort of alleyway between 2 of the Buildings which was a bit of a wind-trap. On the way back up, (you probably guessed) Donnas Wig blew off. I thought, *"Oh Shit!!!"* and chased the Hairy escapee back down the alleyway. Of course, every time I almost had it, `WOOSH`, it was off again. I eventually apprehended the aforementioned escapee and was thinking, *"My God. Donna must be so upset or embarrassed"* but, silly me. She was doubled over Laughing. I said to her that I thought she would be a tad upset about what had just happened and she replied, (while still Laughing) *"You kidding`? Watching you running after that and it kept blowing away from you is the funniest thing I've seen in ages"*

She couldn't wait to go home and call everyone about it. While having her Chemo session she was still Laughing and telling the Nurses and other Chemo receiving patients, all of them having a right good Laugh. When we got home she was on the phone calling everyone to tell them about it. She was still Laughing while on the phone for well over an hour. While she was having a Laugh `at my expense` I went into the Kitchen to make her a Cuppa. I Smiled but, also cried, not because of the `Wig-chasing` scenario but, because it had been the first time in a long time that I saw her so happy and to hear her Laugh again was so special. For the rest of the year, 2010 she had both good and bad days. Nearing the end of the year she was prescribed `A new Cancer treating` drug that apparently concentrated on killing the Cancerous cells and preventing the Cancer from spreading. We had an appointment back at `The Beatson`, (Cancer treatment centre of the Gartnavel Hospital in Glasgow.) It had been advertised as the `New Miracle Drug` in the fight against Cancer.

For Donna, it seemed to be working. She had finished her Chemo treatment and was feeling great. Her Hair started to grow back and she noticed it was growing back kind of Curly and Wavy. She said, *"When I was a wee Lassie I always wanted my Hair like this and ma`h Mammy told me that Ah had to eat ma`h crusts o ma`h pieces to get curly Hair. All Ah had to do wiz get Cancer."*

A sometimes weird sense of humour I know.

We started to look forward to a nice Christmas as Donna was feeling quite good and believing that this `miracle` drug was working because her last appointment at the `Beatson` the Doctor told her that her Tumour had reduced in size by over 60%. And she did not have to come back for a check-up for 4 Month.

All was well until I got a phone call from my young Brother, Tony. He was calling from the Hospital in Milton Keynes. Like our Brother Danny, Tony had moved there also. He said he was just calling to ask how Donna was and the fact that we both hadn't been in touch for about 2 Month so he fancied a `blether` with his Big Brother. We spoke for about a half hour and I told him about how well Donna was doing and discussed what a Beautiful Funeral that Mum had back in January. I asked why he was in Hospital and he told me that, because he suffered from Arthritis (at such an early age) he had been on this

Medication that said in the small print, `Can sometimes cause damage to the Lungs`, however it was only a 0.5% of this occurring. *"Guess what?"* He asked. I said, *"Surely you're not one of the 0.5%?"*. *"I am indeed. Just my Luck. Better chance of winning the Lottery"*. I asked him what damage had been done to his Lungs and he told me that this Medication he had been on has caused a Fungus-like lair on his Lungs. *"Can they fix it?"* I asked. *"I hope so, I'm sick of the Tea in here."* He then said, *"Oh!! Here she comes. The wee Tea Lady. I'll call you soon. If I'm showing no improvement in my recent x-ray they are going to give me a wee blast of Chemo tomorrow. Anyway, take care Bro, and look after Donna."*

That conversation with my Wee Brother, Tony was to be our last. I got a phone call a couple of nights later from my Nephew, Daniel telling me that Tony had passed away. Daniel also told me that Tony had phoned all of his Siblings that same night thinking that he would not survive and just wanted to hear our voices. It was Tony saying goodbye. He didn't want to tell us how bad things were because we were all still grieving about Mum. How brave was my wee Brother to do that?

I had said to my Siblings on the way down to Milton Keynes, (again for a Brother's Funeral) That, in a way, it was a sort of Blessing that Mum had passed when she did, as losing another of her Children would be an overwhelming Heartbreak for her to deal with.

Tony's Funeral had been delayed for a few weeks due to the Cold, Snowy weather and we all arrived the day before. We had arrived in the Morning and were all invited around to our Cousin's house for Breakfast. Later that Day some of us went to `visit` Tony at the Funeral home. He used to take his kids to the Football to support the MK Dons and he was dressed in the team top as he lay in his Coffin.

Because he had been in his Coffin for about 3 weeks due to the delay caused by the aforementioned bad weather, and although he looked peaceful and asleep, he had `Livor Mortis`, (obviously apart from Rigor Mortis) which is the discolouration of a Corpse when the Blood's at the lowest points of the Body and appears in a sort of Purple colour Like a bruise. The `Liver Mortis` in Tony's Corpse was now on his Fingers and the sides of his Handsome face and his Ears.

My Brother Paddy and I went into see him just after Sister Angela had `said goodbye`. As we were leaving Paddy said to me, *"I'll be out in a couple of Minutes. I want to talk to* Tony". Paddy and Tony were very close so I understood why he wanted some time alone with his Big Brother.

I was again asked to write and read out Tony's Eulogy.

Unfortunately, I cannot find a copy of what

I had written but, I know I first referred to his face book profile where he had wrote *"Only the good die young. I must be a Bad-ass."*

I pointed out that he got the first part correct and the second part wrong. He did die young at aged 50 and he was no `Bad-ass`. There wasn't a Bad bone in his Body. I also told the congregation of his Family and Friends about his sense of Humour. After he had passed his driving test in an automatic car, Paddy and I used to call him `Tony-two-pedals`. Tony thought that was hilarious.

He borrowed my 12-string Guitar when I was living in Spain and he turned out to be quite a good Guitarist. He could also sing and whenever he was in company and someone would ask him to get the Guitar out and `give us a song` he would oblige but, before he started singing he would say, *"Okay,* I'll *play this one,* (usually `Where do you go to my Lovely by Peter Sarstedt) but,*

Ah`m nae Neilly." Complimentary or sarcastic? A bit of both I think.

Whenever asked about what he thought of various `Pop-Stars` he usually answered the same. *"Hey, Tony. What dae* yi *think aboot that Singer that sings wi* (whatever pop group)?" He would answer, *"Aye, he's really good but, he's nae Neilly."*

Some of my Nephews still carry on that Trait of Tony`s to this day.

Tony passed away on the 10th of December 2010. Just 11 Month after Mum passed away on the 7th of January 2010.

A horrible year losing 2 dearly Loved members of my Family and worried that in 2011 I would lose another Loved one. My Lovely Donna.

For most of 2011 Donna was mostly feeling fine and didn't have another appointment with her Cancer consultant at the Beaton until May.

We went to the appointment hoping for some good news like maybe the `Miracle

Cancer Drug` she had been prescribed was still working in containing and destroying her Tumour.

Donna told me that even if the Consultant suggested a couple more `Blasts` of Chemo, she would be quite happy with that.

The Consultant told us that all seemed well and the medication seems to be doing it's job and keeping the Tumour `Stable` and Donna didn't have to return for about 4 Month for her next appointment.

We were over the Moon. Donna summed up how she felt by comparing the good news akin to, *"Winning the Lottery"*.

We asked the Consultant if it would be safe enough to go on Holiday because we had been to Turkey the year before and, we wanted to go back but, because of Donnas diagnoses, we weren't sure if we would have another Holiday.   We loved our Holidays.

The Consultant said she didn't see any reason why we shouldn't.

We got home and started looking for a good

Holiday. We eventually decided on going to `Icmeler` in Turkey and booked up for a week in July.

The year before we went to Marmaris in Turkey .

Things were looking good and Donna was feeling great.

I was allowing myself to think that maybe, just maybe, Donna would be a survivor.

But, I received bad news in the second week of June. My Daughters called me to say that their Gran, My Mother-in-Law, had been taken into Hospital. She passed away a day or 2 later on the 14th. (Cancer again) She was a great Woman. Her Great-grandchildren called her `Bingo-Nan`as they had so many `Nans`. My Mum was knows as `Wee Irish Nan` My Son-in-Law's Mum was called, `Nessie-Nan` and my ex-Wife was called, `Nan`.

This time my Daughter, Connie wrote the Eulogy in the form of a Poem but, I read it out with my 3 Daughters standing beside me. They were obviously Grieving as much as I was having lost both their Grans, and a beloved Uncle in so short a time.

`Bingo-Nan` and my Mum, `Wee Irish Nan`, turned out to be the best of Friends and were as thick as Thieves even though, Mary, my ex Wife and I had divorced a lifetime ago.

Mary's Brother, Peter was also very good Friends with my Brother Tony.

When I returned home after the Funeral Donna said to me, *"You really need this Holiday after what you have gone through in the past year or so. Where do you hide all that Grief?"* I said, *"I've got to handle it and, although I'm Heartbroken, it is nothing to what you went, and are still going through after losing Wee John. I must get the strength from you"*.

Donna and I were very close but, we were a lot closer after all the Heartbreak we both had to go through.

Chapter 18

Long lost Sister.

About a week before our first trip to Turkey in 2010, Donna received a letter from the `Salvation Army` asking if she was `The Donna Love` the youngest Child of Hugh and Jessie Love. She called the number supplied and was told that they had received a request from a `Maureen Love` from Maidenhead who was looking for her long lost Siblings. It was indeed Donna`s long lost oldest Sister who, for whatever reason, was brought up in England by her Aunt. They hadn't seen one another for over 20 years when Maureen had travelled up to Paisley for wee John's Funeral. They were soon chatting on the phone and trying to work out when and where they could meet up in either Scotland or England. Donna told her that we were off to Marmaris in Turkey soon and would she like to meet up there. She said, *"I'll get Neil to go online and book you into the same Hotel as us."* I went ahead and booked her flight and the same Hotel for the same day that we would be arriving.

Looking forward to our `unexpected Holiday in 2011, Donna said, *"I'm so happy that we can go on Holiday again. I never thought it would happen"*. She called her Sister, Maureen to ask if she wanted to meet up again but, Maureen had made other arrangements for the date we were going.

Off we went to Turkey and we had a Lovely time but, I noticed Donna`s demeanour. She was really having a nice time but, I got the feeling like she was treating it as her last. She told me that she could have spent another week and that we should have booked up for a 2-week Holiday. The strange thing about that comment is that, on every Holiday we had been on and, we had been on a lot, she had always said, *"I really enjoyed that but, a week was plenty.*" I was more of a 10-day or fortnight Holiday person. On this Holiday however, it was the only time she had ever wished for more than a week.   Did she know or sense something?

While on that Holiday I could not help but reminisce of our time living in Santa Ponca. Donna did not need to work but, being `Donna`, she didn't want to lay by the pool everyday and offered her services as a Cleaner for private apartments and small Bars. She done very well from it and was in high demand. So much so that she had to limit her time to 3 jobs a day. At one point she could have done 5, 6 or more jobs a day. She was always a good hard worker.
We both Loved to welcome Family and Friends who used to visit. Donna`s Sister, Rita and Friend, Nancy paid a few visits.

Others were Donna`s other Sister, Jean and, other Friends, June and, Flo. The first of my Family to visit were my Brother, Joe and his Wife, Rena and then later my Mother, Sister, Mary and Brother, Brian. I of course had my 3 Daughters, Theresa, Lynn and Connie over to visit and also my Nephew, Daniel.

Dad was supposed to come over along with Mum in 1991 but, sadly that was the year he passed away. Mum came over with Joe, Rena and Sister Mary.

We stayed in a private apartment block so there were no Holiday-makers with their Kids running about down by the Pool. This was perfect for Brother, Joe as he was first in the Pool every morning at 8.30am. It was also perfect for Mum as she had never been in a Swimming Pool before.

Joe bought her `Water-wings` and she Loved it. Aged 68-years and her first time in a Pool. When she returned home she went for Swimming lessons and learned how to swim.

When Joe first came over he was quite impressed by my knowledge (although limited) of the Spanish Language. So much so when he returned home he started attending Night classes to learn Spanish. He came back over the following year and while out for a small Afternoon libation we went into my Friend, Pepe`s bar, `The Oasis`. I asked what everyone wanted and Joe said, *"I'll get these, Neil. I am going to order the drinks in Spanish."* I said, *"No problemo. Please do"*.

Joe approached the Bar and asked Pepe for, *"Dos semillas de Cerveza y un uno de Naranja por favor, Pepe."* (Two half Beers and an Orange juice, please, Pepe)

Both myself and Pepe were well impressed. After pouring the drinks Pepe said to Joe, *"Tu Espanol es muy bueno, Joe"*. Joe then turned to me and asked, *"What did he say?"* I laughed and told him, *"Pepe said your Spanish is very good"*.

Like Joe, I found that the better you get at speaking Spanish,   the Spaniard you are conversing with assumes that you are quite fluent and feels comfortable replying at their natural `speed`, which is a lost faster than the way Scottish speak so, quite hard to understand them.

Donna said that she was good at `Supermarket Spanish` as she knew the Spanish for Meat, Bread, Sugar and other food essentials.

In 2014 my Sister, Mary paid for us both to go back for a wee visit. We went for a Fortnight and had a Lovely time. One night sitting having a drink on the Balcony we were reminiscing about the last time she had been here along with Mum, Joe and Rena. I said to her, *"Mary. Do you realize that you are now the same age as Mum was when she was here? 68-years-old."* When we were there Mary suggested that I should try and secure a few gigs and live there again. "I think you would Love to be living out here again." She was of coarse correct. I would indeed Love to be back living there but, I don't think I could work 7 nights a week anymore. It's not so much the age I am now but, having Diabetes is a concern.

Chapter 19

In 2015 Brother, Joe and Wife, Rena, Sisters, Mary and Kathleen and I, all met up in Santa Ponca. I paid another visit in May of 2017 and then in September we all met up again in Benidorm, only this time we were joined by Brothers, Paddy and Brian and their Wives. We are thinking about making it an annual event.
Lots of happy memories about our time in Santa Ponca came flooding back to me while Donna and I were on, what was to be our last Holiday together in Turkey. Nearing the end of the weeks Holiday Donna said to me, *"We will come back in September. What do you think?"*

I said, *"I'm up for that"*. And then she said the strangest thing, *"Do you promise we will be back?"* I said, *"Of coarse. Why shouldn't we? "Just as long as you keep your Promise that we will return"* she answered. I thought it strange that she would make me promise but, I realized some time later what she meant.

We returned home and got back to our usual routine of me doing some gigs throughout the week, and Donna out tending to her   much Loved Garden. She never wasted a ray of Sunshine when it came to her Garden. It was a hobby of sorts that she only discovered she had a talent for after we returned from Santa Ponca. I do not know where it came from but, suddenly it was there. Donna and Sister Maureen had a regular chin-wag over the phone every Monday at 12.30pm in the afternoon and the main subject was their Gardens and what plants they had planted and how said Plants were coming on. It was the same whenever we would visit my Mother's and, after kissing Mum goodbye, I would go and start up the Car but, I usually had to sit waiting for Donna for about 15 minutes while she and Mum discussed Mum's latest plant or Hanging-basket in the front Garden. They Loved their `Botanical Banter` with each other as they were two Ladies who discovered that they had this Botanical talent that they hadn't realized until about the same time as one and other. Mum actually win the `Best Garden` award a few times.

Donna suggested to her Sister Maureen that she would get me to video her showing her Garden and explaining all the work she had been doing in it and send her the DVD. When filming Donna showing off her Beautiful Garden I was amazed as to her knowledge of the plants, bushes and Flowers she was describing as I filmed. She was coming out with the names of each Flower or plant with, not only the English name but, also the Latin name. I asked her ,*"How the Hell did you know all that?"* and she said, *"I have been reading up about `Gardening` and stuff and I, somehow remember. I am surprised myself."* Turns out that one of her Grandparents had been a very good Gardener of whom she never knew about until her Sister told her.

We decided not to book the `other` weeks Holiday in Turkey until after Donna`s next appointment with her Cancer Consultant. On the day of her appointment we were feeling quite confident as we drove into the Beatson Cancer Centre in Glasgow. So much so that I was telling Donna that, as soon as we get back from the appointment I would go online and book our Holiday. Unfortunately, after what the Consultant told us, we knew then that there would be no other week in Turkey, nor any other Holiday together.
The Consultant told us that, although the

`Miracle Drug` was indeed preventing the Cancer from spreading, In Donna`s case, it was prescribed too late. The Cancer had already spread.

A Lovely Summers Evening in August. I had been downstairs to the `Balnagowan Bar` for a couple of Pints and decided to go up to the Flat and grab a few Beers from the Fridge and drink them down in the back Garden.

Donna was still feeling quite well at this time despite the Cancer destroying her from within. I checked on her and she was in Bed reading one of her Books. I told her what I was doing and asked her how she was feeling. *"I feel okay"* She said. I said to her that I would only be about a half hour. After all that had happened in the past year or so, and was still happening, I found having a quiet drink in Donna`s Beautiful Garden, especially on a nice Summers

Evening, somehow helped me to try and understand all the recent trauma. I took two Bottles of Becks from the Fridge, gave Donna a goodnight Kiss and headed down to the Garden.

While sitting with a Beer in Hand I had a Smile on my Face, (or was it a Smile in my Mind?) just admiring the work and Love she had put into this one time ordinary `back court` to change it into such a Beautiful, Serine place that looked even more Lovely on that Moonlit night.

I was just opening my second Beer when I looked up and there was Donna standing there in her Housecoat and a couple of Beers in her Hand. *"I thought you maybe want some company and possibly, a Wee blether?"*

"I knew you would probably want another Beer so, I brought you one down, and one for myself", she said while Smiling and wiping away a Tear from my Eye that she had noticed.

I said to her, *"I couldn't think of anyone I would rather have a drink and a Wee blether with."*
We sat and talked about what Loved ones we had lost and how we would miss them. Donna then looked at me and said, *"Neil. We have both had Heartache but, at the moment, my Tears are for you. You have lost 3 Loved ones in the past year and you know that I will be the next one you will lose. It is not yet over for you."*
On hearing Donna say those words, I just broke down. Donna got off her chair and put her Arms around me and Said, *"I may be gone soon, Neil but, I will always be with you. I promise."*
To this day, those words from Donna still give me comfort.

Chapter 20

As the Days and Weeks went on I could see Donna getting weaker. She would get up in the Morning and feel fine throughout most of the Day usually till about 6 or 7 o'clock. She would suddenly feel very week and Nauseous and had to be helped into Bed. It was at this time that we started getting visits from the Wonderful McMillan Nurses.

For a while it was the same, feeling okay through the Day and the complete opposite after Tea-time.

This went on for a number of Weeks until it got to the stage where it was an effort for her to get out of Bed at all.

There was the odd couple of nights when she wasn't feeling too bad and I would help her out of Bed so she could watch a bit of Television or just sit looking out the Window at the People on the street going about their business.

Donna`s Friend, Nancy was a regular visitor and was a great help to me on Donna`s bad days. She would help with getting Donna to and from the Toilet, doing some housework and cooking. Nancy and

Donna had been Friends since Childhood. By this time I had given up my regular gigs at the Loch Awe and Inversnaid Hotels. I was too scared that if Donna had a turn for the worse, I would be too far away. My nearest gig was an hour and a half drive away from Home.

I decided to give up the gigs to be there for Donna as one night I had been sitting with her in what I called, `my office`. (Donna called it `her Kitchen`) She asked me to help her back to bed. I walked her through to the Bedroom and she sat on the side of the Bed. *"Do you want tucked in"* I asked. She said, *"No. I'll just sit for a while. Come back in 5* minutes and *help me in."* I asked if she wanted a cuppa and she said to bring one in when I come back. I told her, *"I'll leave the Bedroom door and my office door open."* *"Kitchen Door you mean"* she answered sarcastically.

I went through to the office….sorry….Kitchen and put the Kettle on. About a minute later I went through to ask her if she wanted a Sandwich or a Biscuit with her Tea.

I got the fright of my Life. Donna was sat on the Bed with her Arm stretched out trying to beckon me to her.

She couldn't Breath nor even catch a Breathe. She grabbed hold of me while she was waving her other Hand in front of her Mouth as if to try and get some air.

The only thing I could think to do was grab the Fan that we used when she had been feeling too Hot, and hold it about a foot from her Face. Thankfully, it worked as it forced her to take a deep, gasping flow of air into her Lungs. "You're okay!! You're okay!! I said while she held me tight and shaking with the awful fright she had just had. I told her, *"Just relax and Breathe. You will be okay. I'm here with you."*

We sat for a few minutes with me holding on to her like a Father with his frightened Child.

She then said to me, *"Neil. I thought that was it. I was frightened because I don't want to die gasping for air. I want to go in my Sleep."* She then said, *"I couldn't call you and, thinking I was about to go, I just wanted you to be with me and holding my Hand. Whatever way I go please be with me and hold my Hand."* I said, *"I promise you. I'll be with you. I will be holding your Hand."* She drifted off to sleep and I gently tucked her in. I sat with her for about an hour just watching her sleep, and holding her Hand. For the next week I could hardly sleep too frightened in case she went without me. The Stress was starting to tell on me now. My Face was drawn in and I had no appetite. I did not want to leave Donna`s side.

One Evening we had a visit from the McMillan Nurse and it was a rare night that Donna was feeling okay. Donna told the Nurse that I had been invited to a night out, a memorial night behalf of my dear Friend, Denis McBride who had fallen victim to this horrible Serpent of Satan known as Cancer some years before. The same Serpent that had taken my Mum and Dad, my 2 Brothers and my Mother-in-law and now well on it's way to taking my Soul mate, Donna.

I insisted that I would not leave Donna`s side but, Donna was insisting that I go. *"All your music Friends from way back will be there, Neil. You should go and have a catch-up with them. And, it's for your Friend, Denis."*
I was still adamant that I was not leaving Donna`s side for a minute then the Nurse said, *"Listen Neil. Why don't you go for a couple of hours and meet your Friends? Donna will be fine and I'll sit with her until you get back. You also need some respite as you are starting to look a bit stressed out. You have been through a lot in the past year or so from what Donna has told me."*
I reluctantly agreed to go but, I said, *"Only*

for an hour."

The Nurse seen me to the door and told me, *"Donna has been really worried about you. She has noticed that you have looked stressed out recently and told me about you not having a chance to Grieve properly for your Mum and Brother. Go and meet your Friends. Donna really wants you to have a break."*

Typical Donna. More worried about me rather than what she was going through.

I got a Taxi to `The Swan` pub and it was indeed nice to meet up with some old musician Friends, some I hadn't seen for years, but, I must have phoned Donna every 10 minutes or so. She eventually told me, *"Don't phone again. I'm fine. Do what you're told or I will find the energy to kick your Arse when you get back."*

Her Humour had not diminished one iota, unlike her Health.

Back in `The Swan` the evening was going down well with all the guys and Girls going on stage and playing and singing as a tribute to our mutual much missed and much Loved Friend, Denis. I was standing having a pint with one or two of my old Friends when one of them said, "Yes!!! There's `Jukebox` just come in." `Jukebox` was our Friend and Paisley Legend, Willie (jukebox) Matthews. I approached `Jukebox` to say hello as I hadn't seen him for a few years. (Jukebox was instrumental in getting me the work in Spain as he was the one who put my name forward to the Radio Clyde DJ, Emperor Roscoe who had called me offering me the work out there. The day Donna and co were all packed for Rothesay)

Jukebox always had this great White Toothy Smile but, when I got close to him he only had one Tooth. I looked at him and said, *"Willie, how you doing mate? What happened to that lovely smile?".* He then told

me, *"I've only got a few Month left, mate. I got CANCER. Thought I'd come here for a wee song while I can."*
Yet again, the Evil Serpent of Satan never stops.

My Brother, Paddy gave me a run home from The Swan that night and when I got in I thanked the Nurse for sitting with Donna. She said that she was more than happy to have kept Donna company. She said to me as I seen her out, *"Donna is quite a Lady. She had me in stitches talking about your life together. And that story of you chasing after her Wig? Oh, that just floored me."* I said to Donna, *"Well. The Nurse enjoyed your company it seems."* *"Aye, we had a nice wee night. How was your night?"* She asked. I said I had quite a good night and it was great to catch up with some old Friends. I never told her about `Jukebox`.
She said that every time I called her she had

said, *"Shit !! No` again ! Geiz-a-brek. Every 2 minutes? Really?"* and the Nurse pissed herself laughing every time.

I said, *"I was just worried and was checking to see if you were alright."* *"I know that"* she said but, *"I wanted you to have a couple of hours at least, not worrying about me. You needed a break, Neil. Anyway, I'm not going anywhere soon."*

We sat and spoke for a while before going to Bed and I asked her what she had been telling the Nurse that made her Laugh so much. *"Just various things, good and bad that we had experienced in our time together."* she said.

For example, the time her Friend, June Byers came to visit us in Santa Ponca. June had arrived and we picked her up from the Palma Airport but, she and others on the same flight from Glasgow Airport, (which, incidentally is in Paisley, not Glasgow) had no luggage to retrieve. The Airline they had travelled with had put their luggage on a different flight. They had to leave their `Holiday address` so as their luggage could be delivered to them as soon as possible. June was only over for a week and her luggage arrived the day before she was heading back home.

Luckily, Donna and June were similar in size so June dressed in some of Donna`s clothes, and Underwear for the week. For some unknown reason Donna had a drawer full of Red Sexy Knickers and wore a pair of these Red pants just about every night. I'm sure it was nothing to do with my preference of Red Bras and Knickers but, more Donna`s preferred Colour of underwear.

Anyway, the day June arrived Donna took her to my gig in `Caesars` Hotel. I was singing away to a floor full of Holiday-time dancers and having another great night. It was a very busy Hotel and that night it was full of `just arrived` guests. After having them up dancing non-stop for about 15 minutes with a medley of Rock`n`Roll, I took a break. I said my usual `taking a break` catch-phrase of, *"I am taking a 5 minute break for 10 minutes. Be back in half an hour."*

I went and sat with Donna and June for the aforementioned `break` and June said, *"Neil, that's the first I've heard you singing since we all used to go to the `Knights of St. Columbus Club` a good few years back. Really enjoying it."*

I said, *"Thank you, June. By the way, has your luggage arrived yet?"* She said, *"No. Not yet but, I hope to get it tomorrow."*

I went back on-stage and, because it was newly arrived guests, I thought that I would introduce my Lovely Wife, Donna and her dear Friend, June.

"Ladies and Gentlemen. I would like you all to say hello to my Lovely Wife and her Friend, Donna and June, who are both wearing Red Knickers by the way."

The look Donna gave me was enough to make me think, *"Oh-Oh, I'm not going to see those Red Knickers tonight."*

We were having a bit of a laugh reminiscing and Donna also told the Nurse of one time we had fallen out for whatever reason, as Loved ones do.
I was in a hurry to leave for my gig at the Loch Awe Hotel one Saturday night and this was about a week after we had fallen out. (we never, ever fell out for long) Donna had forgot to put the Washing into the tumble-dryer and I needed fresh underpants. She grabbed a pair of Boxers from the Washing machine to put over the radiator but, they would never have been dry enough by the time I had to leave for work.
She looked in the bottom drawer of my `underwear` cabinet and found another pair only these were Y-Fronts. I quickly put them on when I came out the Shower and

said to Donna, *"You're a life-saver. What would I do without you? "You would have to go to work wearing Dirty pants"* She replied. I jumped in the Car and started my 75 mile drive to the Hotel but, as I approached the Erskine Bridge I noticed that I was `burning up` in my nether regions. I was very uncomfortable and thinking, *"Whit the F##k? M`ah Baws are on fire."* They were getting worse the more I carried on driving but, just at the North end of Dumbarton I thought, *"Can't handle this anymore. Need to go home in case I need an Ambulance."* I called the Hotel to say that I couldn't make it as I had been in a minor Car crash and had to wait on the Police attending. There was no way I was going to call the Hotel and say, *"Sorry, canny make it tonight. M`ah baws are on fire"* I got home and immediately ran into the Bathroom and filled up the Water basin with Cold Water, stood on my tip-toes and submerged my delicate Crown Jewels into the soothing   coldness of the Basin. Donna, with a worried look on her face asked, *"What's wrong? Are you okay?"* I said, *"M`ah Baws are burning. Ah don't know whit`s wrong."*

After about 10 minutes the burning was easing and I went into the Living room where Donna was sitting and said to her, *"I don't know what happened. I maybe need to call the Doctor tomorrow, or tonight if it comes back."*

Donna was sitting quietly and I was wondering why she was not as much concerned about the situation than I was. I then noticed a `Guilty` grin on her face and said to her, *"You know what this is, don't you?"*

She then explained to me, while laughing, that she had rubbed Curry and Chile powder into the crutch of a pair of my Pants at the time we had the `fall-out` the week before.

Another time I was leaving for a gig when she said to me, *"Eh!! Before ye go, leave yer Fiver for the Provy man. I had to pay yours last week."* I told her I only had a tenner on me. She said, *"Ah`ve got a Fiver change here"* I went into my pocket and pulled out `a Fiver` and immediately said to her, *"Right!! You give me that Fiver first. "*, *"Naw, you give me the Tenner first."* she replied. I said, *"Okay. After Three we swap at the same time. Okay?" "Okay"* she said. *"ONE. . .TWO. . .THREE".* We swapped notes but Donna didn't notice that we had just swapped Fivers. I gave her a goodbye Kiss left for the gig with a Cheeky but, Guilty smirk on my face. She never found out about it until I told her years later down at the Pool in Santa Ponca but, I gave her 6,000 Pesetas (£30) to say sorry. She still pushed me in the Pool.

We had another few nights like that just

talking about this and that but, we were avoiding the thought of our good lives together being taken away from us.

One night Donna said to me, *"Neil. What's that Prayer? You know the one where you're asking God why you have to leave the Life you have behind and you don't feel ready to go?"* I said, *"Don't think so but, I'll Google it."* I then said, *"Why that Prayer? Is that the way you feel?* She said, *"Yes. I have been so Happy with you and I'm Happy for Stephen and his Lovely Wife, Tanya, and, of coarse Wee John*, (her Grandson) *Victoria,* (her Granddaughter) *and `the Bump`.* (her unborn Granddaughter) *I'm just not ready to go yet and leave you all behind."*

I `Googled` high and low but, I could not find such a Prayer or any Prayer similar to it. I told Donna that I couldn't find it so she asked me, *"Could you write a Prayer with those Sentiments? I know you could."*

I told her I would see what I could do and after about an hour, I had written this:

`DONNA`S LAST PRAYER`

`Help me accept`

I cannot fault this Life I've had, sometimes Good and sometimes Bad.
Other People have had it tough, for these unfortunates Life's been Rough.
With Loving Family I've been Blessed, my Husband, Friends, for me the best.
Lovely places I have been that other People have never seen.

I've seen many People Young and Old, whose Life to me seemed hard and Cold.
A Child with Parents that do not care. A Parent with Child that's never there.
Who do they have when they're in Pain?
Who do they have to keep them Sane?
Who will be there to shed a Tear when they are Sadly no longer here?
So, tell me Lord why I'm so Sad, to leave

behind all that I've had?
I know that soon I will have to go but, do I want to? The answer's no.
I hope Dear Lord that it is true, when I have gone I'll be with you.
I do not know Lord if you are there but, if you are, Please hear my Prayer.

`Grant me strength to comprehend, why my contented Life has got to end.
Help me accept the fate I face, with understanding, Pride and Grace.
Please help me keep my Head up high, when it's time to say Goodbye.
I am grateful for the Life I've had, that's why to leave, it makes me Sad.
Help me walk this one more Mile, so I can leave my Loved ones with a Smile`.

She Cried when she read it, as did I when I wrote it.

"Are you hungry at all, Donna? I'm going to

make   a bit of Lunch," "Not really," She answered, *" but, I'll maybe have a wee plate of Scrambled Egg if you help me up to the Kitchen"* I helped her up to her Chair in my office. . . Sorry, Her Kitchen and she sat reading her book. *"What you making?"* she asked. I said, *"I'm having the same as you. Scrambled Egg. You wanting a slice of Toast with yours?"* *"No"* she answered, *"Just the Egg, thanks."*

As I was making the, `Huevos Revueltos`, a song came on the Radio. *"Oh!! That's the song I want on at the end of my Funeral,"* she said. The song was `Enjoy yourself. It's later than you think` by Prince Buster.

A great wee `catchy` song basically telling you to have a good time before it's too late. *"For your Funeral?,"* I asked. *"Aye"* she replied, *"But make it the last song as people are leaving. I want them to leave with a smile on their face."* Typical Donna. Always thinking of others.

The other 2 songs she picked were `All

things Bright and Beautiful`, (her favourite since Childhood) and the English version of, `Time to say Goodbye`.

I said I would record them onto a CD later on but, she asked if I could do it today. *"There's no hurry."* I told her. *"Can you just do it,"* she asked, *"I can relax a bit knowing that it's done, and anyway, I want to listen to them."*

I said, *"Okay. I'll do it after my `Huevos Revueltos` but, we got plenty time to sort out these things."* *"You don't know that, Neil."* She said. *"And will you give it a miss with that Spanish gobbledygook shit?"*

She was always a very organised Woman. She had actually paid for her Funeral after she found out that there was nothing that could be done to help her.

She hadn't finished her Scrambled Egg and asked me to help her back to Bed. I asked how she was feeling. *"Not very good."* she answered.

This had been the way for a few weeks now.

One minute she is fine, laughing and talking away, the next, very week and listless. Later that day she had another `breathless episode`. I turned the Fan on and held it up to her Face again. She caught her breathe and held on to me. *"I hate this. When that happens it's so frightening. It's so damn Frightening!!!"* Holding her close and wiping her Tears I told her,

"Shhhh. You'll be fine. When the Angels come for you, you will be Sleeping but, that won't be for a while yet,"

"I wish they would hurry up, Neil." she said. *"I'm getting really tired of it all."*

She had indeed been fighting so hard. She knew that even on the days she felt quite good, she knew it could change at any time. That must have been mentally exhausting for her let alone the Pain that would suddenly hit her.

She always had the attitude that she was `Living` with Cancer and not `Dying` with Cancer but, it now seemed as though that

Bastard disease was starting to get the upper hand.

As the weeks went on she was becoming more and more Bed-ridden. When she had to go to the Toilet, she had to be `wheeled` in to the Bathroom which was less than 3 yards away from the Bedroom. I, the Nurse or Nancy, would also give her a Bed-Bath most days. She had very little strength or fight left in her.

I would sit at the side of the Bed and watch her Sleep for hours. I was so afraid that she would wake up gasping for Breath as I knew she was so frightened of her Life ending that way. I was now hoping that when it happens, then it happens the way Donna hoped for, to go peacefully in her Sleep.

One Morning I was making myself some Breakfast when I heard Donna call on me. I went through to her and noticed she was looking a bit more `awake` and Brighter. I said, *"How you feeling Love? You look a lot* better today." She said, *"Aye, I'm okay-ish. Actually feeling a bit peckish. You want to make me some of that `Scramble-o Eggy-o`? or whatever you call it in Spanish."* Sounded more like the Funny Lady I love.

She managed to finish off the `Scramble-o Eggy-o` and said she enjoyed that. I asked her if she wanted to try getting out of Bed and watching a bit of Telly. She said, *"Aye. Sounds like a plan but, just sit me at the Window and never mind the Telly."*

For the first time in ages, although quite weak, she was more like her old self again. She called her Sister, Maureen and, Friend, Nancy for a wee blether. It was nice to hear her a Laugh a few times while on the phone. I had been in my office, . . . Sorry, the Kitchen while Donna was on the phone.

At one point I heard my name mentioned so I eavesdropped in on her `Blether` and I heard her say, *"Aye, Nancy. Neil has been brilliant. He's doing all he can to help me. I would be lost without him. He's my Rock."*

(or words to that effect)
To hear her say that was humbling and gave me a lump in my throat.

Chapter 21

Donna had now been, `okay-ish` for a few more days, and during those few days we had a good wee `Chin-wag` and a deep conversation or two about our time together.
She asked me if I could remember when she lost a Tooth which the Dentist had removed so as to give her a better Crown on her Bottom row that would give her a perfectly straight line of Teeth and compliment her already Beautiful Smile. She said, *"You wanted me to keep the Tooth for some reason and give it to you."* I said, *"Yes, I remember but, can you remember why?"*
Of course she remembered. She knew that whenever any of my Grandchildren, had lost a Tooth, their Mum would put them on

the phone to ask Granddad if he could phone his good Friend, the Tooth Fairy. (aka, Granddad) who would send a letter from her home in `Dingily-Dell` thanking them for their Tooth and tell them that the Tooth would be taken to the Dingily-Dell Fairy-dust factory and it would be ground-down to make more Fairy-dust and, of course they would find payment for it under their Pillow.

Donna came back from the Dentist with her recently removed Tooth and gave it to me and asked, *"Are you going to give this to the Tooth Fairy?"* (Who's name was actually, `Fairy Nuff`)

I said, *"Of coarse. She will write you a letter thanking you for it. As she does with the Grandchildren,"*

As promised, Donna awoke in the Morning and found a `Fiver` under her Pillow.

"Where's my letter from Fairy Nuff?" she asked. I told her that the Postman had been while she was still asleep but, I've got it

here. "You want to read it?" *"Aye"* she `demanded`.

I gave her the Letter from Fairy Nuff, the Tooth Fairy and it read.:

Dear Donna. Thank you ever so much for your Tooth donation to our Fairy Dust production factory here in Dingily-Dell. As you may, or may not know, we grind down all tooth donations to make Fairy Dust but, unfortunately, the Tooth you donated is far too old and decrepit for Fairy Dust but, we can use it as a Hale-stone during a Hale-storm over Paisley in September of this year. Thank you again for your kind donation. Signed, Fairy Nuff. Chief Tooth Fairy."

We had a good laugh remembering that `letter` from the Tooth Fairy and then she asked me if I remember the note/poem I had left one Morning asking her to leave me the money for 10 fags.

I had come home one night and had hardly any Cigarettes and not enough money in my pocket to buy any in the Morning. I did not want to wake her up as she was up early in the Morning and was not a great sleeper at the best of times. This is the note/poem she was referring to:

`90p to my name. Not many Fags till you get hame.
The price of Ten, I do not know.
Please help me out before you go.
If this for me you can cater, I'll do without my Morning Paper.
10 Fags I know is not many but, without your help,
I won't have any.
If this you do for your Man,
When you get home, I'll give you wan.`
She left me the price of 20 Cigarettes.

The reason I can remember these poems and letters, word for word is that Donna kept them all. I found them in one of her Handbags.

Donna had been feeling `not too bad` for about 3 Days but, then, out of the Blue, she was really ill again. She was so ill that I decided to call the Doctor. He was at the house in less than an hour. He checked Donna over and then said to me and Nancy (who I also called) *"I think we should get her to Hospital as I think she has a slight Chest infection. We need to have her on Oxygen."* The Ambulance arrived and the paramedics and secured her in a Stair Chair. They got her downstairs and into the Ambulance. Nancy went in the Ambulance with her and I followed in my Car.

She was examined again at the Hospital and settled in Bed with the Oxygen tubes gently supplying Air through her Nose. The Doctor told me that she did indeed have a `mild` Chest infection but, although it is `mild`, it would be very difficult for Donna to fight it off in her condition.

I said to Nancy that I didn't think she would make it past the Weekend. Nancy agreed and said to me, *"You just need to psych yourself up to be ready for the inevitable. We all will."*

I continued to sit with Donna as she drifted in and out of Sleep. At one point she said to me, *"Neil. Away home and get something to eat, and try and get some sleep. I'll be okay. If anything happens the Nurse will phone you."*
She also said that she would probably Sleep the rest of the Day and Night anyway.
For a couple of Days there wasn't much change in her condition. Every visit she would talk for a while and then drift off to sleep.
I had thought that she wouldn't see out the Weekend but, when I arrived at the Hospital on the Monday, I was pleasantly surprised to see her sitting up on the Bedside Chair and chatting and Laughing with one of the Nurses.
"Wow!" I said. *"You're looking better. How*

you feeling?"

"I feel fine" she said. *"I even had some Breakfast this Morning and the Doctor told me that the `mild` Chest infection was gone. He said I can maybe go Home soon."*

I could not believe the Strength and Fight that this Wonderful Woman of mine possessed.

Through the ongoing week she had many visitors.

Her Aunty Jean, Niece, Alison Love, Nancy, June.

Her Son Stephen and his Wife, Tanya, Grandkids, Victoria and wee John and many more including my Sisters, Kathleen, Theresa, Angela, and Brother, Paddy.

I surprised her on the Thursday by bringing her late Sister, Rita's Grandsons, Dean and Liam. When she saw them her face lit up and she said, *"Awe, ma`ah boys."*

On the Friday evening of November 26th, 2011 I was up to visit along with my Sisters, Kathleen and Theresa, and Brother, Paddy and his Wife, Margaret.

I was so glad to be able to visit as for most of the Day I had been to my Doctor that Morning complaining of an itchy rash on my Back and Shoulder. It turned out I had `Shingles.` My GP said that I could not go anywhere near the Hospital because of this. I asked him, "When can I go up? How long before I get rid of `Shingles`?" He told me, "6 to 4 Weeks." I told him that my Wife was in Hospital and, although she might be getting home soon, I need to be with her. *"If she doesn't get let home then, I may never see her again. I have got to go to her."* I said. He told me that he sympathised with me but, for me to go into a Hospital environment with Shingles would be unfair and dangerous for other patients.

As I was driving home from my Doctors I was thinking that there is no way I am not going to the Hospital to visit my Donna. I did not care about anyone `catching` the Shingles off me. All I had to do was make sure that I didn't get too close to Donna in case she got infected.

Donna had been informed by one of the Nurses that I wasn't able to come visit. According to the Nurse, who I spoke to on the phone, Donna was really upset. *"If Neil can't come here to see me then I want to go home now,"* She told the Nurse.

The Ward Sister told Donna, *"Don't worry Donna. I'll give Neil a call."*

The Ward Sister called me at home and said that, as long as the infected area of my Body was not exposed so much that anyone could actually `touch it`, then there was nothing to worry about. She asked, *"Where is your infection?"* I told her, *"On the left side of my Back and mainly on my Shoulder."* She then said, *"I take it you will be wearing a pullover, maybe a vest and wearing a Jacket?* I said, *"Of course. It's November."* *"Okay, I'll tell Donna that you are on your way. I don't think anyone is going to shove their Hand up your Semmit."*

I was over the Moon after that call from the Ward Sister although I was a bit concerned as to why my GP insisted that I couldn't go anywhere near the Hospital.

It didn't matter anyway. I went to see my Lady and she was so pleased that the Ward Sister had said it was okay for me to visit. Donna said, *"I was ready to sign myself out if you were not allowed to visit. Cancer has never stopped us so, what chance the wee diddy Shingles?"*

Visiting time was over and my Sisters gave Donna a goodnight kiss. I always held on for a few minutes after other visitors left, just to have a few minutes alone. She said to me before I left, *"I love to see Kathleen and Theresa visit. I look forward to visiting time to see who has taken the time to come see me but, believe it or not, I'm like a teenager with Butterflies in my Tummy when I see you walk in."*

She also said, *"Always know that I have always Loved you and always will. You have*

always been there for me."
I said, *"I always will Babe."*
As I was leaving the Ward I saw my Sisters speaking to a Nurse that they knew. As I waited for them to finish their conversation with the her, another Nurse went into Donna`s Ward presumably to give out Meds or whatever. When she entered the Ward she pulled back one of the `Curtains` for whatever reason and I saw Donna. She didn't see me as she was sitting up in Bed the way I had left her but, my Heart broke when I saw the Tears run down her Face. I ran back in and gave her a big Cuddle and said, *"You're not alone, Babe. I'll be back tomorrow. Love you."* I wiped her Tears and kissed her Forehead and gave her `that Wink` she always liked. She Smiled and blew me a Kiss as I left the Ward.
I said goodnight to my Sisters and drove home. When home I decided to go downstairs to the Pub and have a cheeky wee Becks or three. I was telling Shirley,

the pub owner who was Friends with Donna, about the whole `Shingles` scenario and how Donna said that she would have signed herself out if I wasn`t allowed to go visit. *"That sounds like my pal, Donna."* Shirley gave me a couple bottles of Cheeky wee Becks to take upstairs with me. As I was sitting drinking the aforementioned wee cheeky chaps, I got a text. The text was sent from Donna and it quite simply read, *"Love you v much. xxxx"* I texted her back saying, *"Love you v   much more. ☺ "* Little did I know that night, that text would be the last ever contact between us.

Saturday, November 26th.   I phoned the Hospital at 10.30am to ask if Donna had a good night and how she was feeling. The Nurse told me that she had been sleeping all night, and was still sleeping. *"Cant you wake her for some Breakfast or maybe a cup of Tea?"* I asked. The Nurse said, *"Unfortunately, no. When we tried she would open her Eyes for a minute or two and then drift off again. We are moving her into a single bed unit for privacy. We think it best that you sit and spend time with her."*

Although I knew that this time would come, I didn't really expect it. I was thinking maybe another Month or so. After thinking how ill she was when taken into Hospital just 10 days before and not expecting her to see that weekend. She came through it and had been bright and chatty since then. So much so that the Doctor said she could go back Home on the Monday.

I was thinking this Woman is Invincible. Meanwhile, my Daughter, Theresa and Husband, George had driven up from Bournemouth to visit George's Parents in Greenock and then visit me on their way back. When Theresa saw how Donna was she told George to go home without her. *"I'll stay here with Dad and Donna."* I was so happy that she decided to stay and help me through this. I told Theresa that. Donna was excited about getting Home. I explained that the night before on the Friday Donna asked me, *"What day is this?"* I said, *"It's Friday. 3 more sleeps and you'll be back in your own Bed."* *"Can't wait for Monday,"* She said.

When I arrived on the Saturday Morning her Niece, Jeanette and her Husband, George had travelled through from Edinburgh to visit her. Donna had been hoping that they would come through. It was sad to see that Donna was more or less Comatose by the time they got there. I thanked them for coming through and told them that I wish that Donna knew you were here. Jeanette said, *"I think she knows, Neil. While we were sitting with her she opened her Eyes briefly and looked at us and Smiled. She knows we are here."*

I was happy to hear Jeanette tell me that as, I was hoping for Donna to wake up, even just for a Minute and see that I was there with her.

Donna had not yet been moved to the one Bed unit thus far. I asked one of the Nurses why, and she told me, with a, `you know what I mean` look in her Eye, *"Room 2 should be available in about an hour."*
I knew exactly what she meant as I had seen a couple of the Porters remove the unfortunate former resident of room 2 contained in the `covered-trolley` earlier. I had done that many times before when I worked in the old Hospital, The R.A.I. Eventually, Donna was moved into `room 2` and I just sat with her for a few Hours. I spoke to her hoping that she could hear me, and knowing that she couldn't answer me. After a while I got a call from my Brother, Paddy asking if I needed anything like Food or Juice if I was going to sit with Donna all day and night.
I said to Paddy to come up and sit with Donna for an hour while I drove to ASDA to get enough bits and bobs. I made sure I

had enough Sandwiches and Juice to keep me fed and Watered while sitting with Donna for however long it would take. My Daughter, Theresa also brought me up some `supplies`.

Paddy and I had `done the Nightshift` sitting with our Dying Mother just over a Year before, and Paddy said, *"I'll keep you and Donna company every night if you want."*

I told him, although he didn't have to, it would be appreciated.

Paddy then left to do the things he had to do like, normal everyday things, go Shopping, have Dinner, yadda, yadda.   He returned to join me on the `nightshift`. We sat with Donna and Paddy spoke about the times Donna helped him out back in the Days when he was a young Married man. How she would pay for his St. Mirren season ticket, (which he always paid back) and various other ways she was always there for him. She also appreciated his sense of humour like on her last Birthday earlier in March 5th, 2011, he and his Wife, Margaret popped up with a Birthday card and a couple of gifts. The first of those gifts was a wee Teddy Bear he purchased from the Pound shop with the writing on it saying, `Thank you`. (I still have Teddy on my Mantle) The other gift was a 20 pack of Cigarettes. Donna, (who was still smoking at the time as there was no point in stopping) said to Paddy, *"You do know that it's Lung Cancer I've got?"* Paddy answered, *"Of course I do. That's why I got you 20 `light` fags. I'm not totally insensitive you know."* Donna thought that was hilarious and said, *"That was nice of you to take my health into consideration. Thanks."*

We sat by Donna`s Bedside the whole night and about 7.30am, Sunday 27th November, Paddy went home for some Breakfast and a Shower. He returned about 2 hours later and sat with Donna so I could do the same.

I returned and sat with Donna the rest of the Day apart from going for a bite to eat or out for a quick cigarette. I would make sure that there was someone to sit with her before doing the aforementioned. This was not a problem as Donna had plenty visitors that day including her Son, Stephen, a couple of her Friends, a couple of my Sisters, and of course, my Daughter, Theresa.

She was never short of visitors.

Night time was upon us and Paddy had returned to sit with me at Donna`s Bedside. I was telling Paddy about the couple of times Donna had the `Breathless` episodes. *"That must have been so scary for both of you."* He said.

I told him it had been very frightening and that I promised Donna that I would be with her, holding her Hand when the time came. *"That's why I hate to leave her Bedside for whatever reason,"* I said. *"I will keep that promise."*

Chapter 21

The last goodbye

The night slowly went by as we also talked about Mum, and Tony. We shared various stories about them both, some sad but, mostly happy memories. Paddy asked me about my Daughters and how they were dealing with everything that had happened in the past year. He said, *"With Mary Mackin, (my Mum-in-law) dying with Cancer in June, the Girls have lost both their Grans, their Uncle Tony and now their Step-Mum, Donna will soon be gone."* I told him that, of course they are suffering but, they said they were more concerned about me and how I was dealing with all this stress. *"Is that why you got the `Shingles` because of the Stress?"* he asked. *"Yes. According to my Doctor, that's why I got them, but, I would gladly swap Donna and take her Cancer."* I replied.

I had fallen asleep with my Head on the side of Donna`s Bed but, still holding her Hand, when Paddy woke me to say he was going home for an hour to get some Breakfast and have a Shower. I said, *"I'll come down to the Car with you. Need to stretch my Legs."* The time was 7.15am. Monday, November 28th. I walked down to the Car park with Paddy and had a quick ciggie before returning to the Ward.

On my return I noticed that Donna was moving her right Arm up and down and to the side as if looking for something. She had hardly moved at all in the last 48 hours. I pressed the Buzzer for the Nurse and then took a hold of Donna`s Hand telling her, *"I'm here Donna. I'm here."* in the forlorn hope that she was waking up. She seemed to settle down after that and I swear that I felt as though she gave my Hand a soft squeeze. The Nurse came in and checked on Donna. As she was checking her Pulse and looking into her Eyes with the beam of a small Torch, I told the Nurse about her movement and that she looked a bit agitated until I spoke to her. The Nurse turned to me and said, *"I'm sorry but, she is about to `go`. I'll leave you alone with her."*

I asked the Nurse why her Arm had been moving and she said, *"You told me she settled down once you spoke to her? She was probably looking for you. She knows you have been with her."*

I sat with Donna for a few more minutes holding her Hand and Stroking her Hair. As I was watching her Life ebb away from her, there were 4 short gasps of Air and her Eyes rolled back. Those Beautiful Eyes she had were now Lifeless.

Monday November 28th at 7.35am. The Love of my Life. My Soul mate. My Beautiful Wife was gone, on the Day she was looking forward to getting Home.

I kept my Promise and had one more Promise to keep.

I remembered Donna telling me about a book she had once read concerning people who had experienced `near Death experience` and how they described being above and looking down on their Body. Some had died while on the operating table and could see the Doctors and Nurses trying to revive them. Some died in an accident like a Car Crash and also seemed to be looking down the carnage and their `remains`.

I don't know why that came into my Mind but, just about a Minute after Donna passed away, I looked up toward the Ceiling just in case she was looking down and could see me holding her Hand. I said to her, *"I hope you can see me, Donna. I'm going to miss you so much but, Wee John will be Happy to have his Mum with him again."*

I thought that I had better phone Donna`s boy, Stephen. I called his number but, I heard it ring out in the Corridor.

He walked into the room and saw me sitting with his Mother with the Tears running down my Face. *"She's gone Son. Your Mum's gone."* I told him she had just passed about 5 Minutes ago. He took hold of her other Hand and leaned over to kiss her Forehead. I said, *"I'll leave you alone with Mum for a few Minutes, Stephen."* I walked out the room and down to the Car Park and I remember feeling sort of Lost and Lonely. My phone rang and it was my Daughter, Lynn calling me from Bournemouth. *"Hi, Dad. Just leaving for work but, I thought I would call you to see how Donna was."* I told her Donna had passed away less than 10-Miutes ago.

"Oh, Dad. I'm so sorry. I wish I was there with you right now. Are you okay?" I said, *" I wish you were here too Love. I'm not okay at the moment but, I will be."*

I called Family and Friends to let them know about Donna, and throughout the rest of the Morning some of them came up to see her and say farewell. The Final farewell of coarse would be at the Funeral.

Although there were a few around Donna`s Bed, I felt like I was in a Bubble and alone. In my Mind I was Icmeler market in Turkey watching Donna haggle the Stall owner for a cheaper price on what she wanted to buy. She usually got her way. One time she said to me while at the Market, *"Oh, Neil. Look at that Lovely Clock. I'm gonna have that."* She asked the stall owner the price of the Clock. *"45 Lira* (just under £10) *Madam."* *"No."* She said. *"I'll give you 30 Lira."* (about £6) He replied, *"30 Lira? No, no, no. It is nice Clock and worth more. I give you for 40."* (about £8) Donna said *"No. Too much"* and slowly walked away. I said to her, *"I thought you really wanted that clock?"* *"I do"* she said. Just then, the stall owner called her back. *"Watch and learn"* she told me with a cheeky wee smirk on her Face. *"Okay*

Madam. I give you for 30 Lira." Donna said, *"I'll give you 25 Lira (£5) but, I will take two."* The stall owner laughed and said, *"Okay. I give you two Clocks for 25 Lira each. How you say in Scotland? You a tough Cookie?"*

My train of thought was disturbed when I heard Paddy say, *"Neil. I'll need to go. Let me know when you are back home and I'll pop up later." "Will do, thanks,"* I answered. Eventually everyone except my Daughter, Theresa had left. My Daughter said, *"We better go Dad and let the Nurses see to Donna."* I reluctantly agreed and gave Donna a final kiss and whispered into her Ear, *"Love you for Eternity, Donna."*

After driving back from the Hospital with my Daughter, I parked the Car and we walked across the Road to my House. Word about Donna had already got around as some of the regulars of the `Balnagowan`, who had been standing outside having a Smoke, came up to me and passed on their Condolences. Many of them knew Donna and were very Fond of her. The owner of the Pub, Shirley, who was Friendly with Donna, popped up to my flat to see me. She had been up to visit Donna in Hospital on the Thursday Afternoon. She said to me, *"I can't believe it, Neil. She looked so well the other Day. She was in a Happy mood."* Shirley had just found out on her return to the Pub after attending the Funeral of one of the regulars.

Chapter 22

I had left Donna's Son, Stephen to arrange his Mum's Funeral and sort out her Money affairs. As I said before, Donna had already paid for her Funeral and she was able to leave some Money for both Stephen and I.

We knew how much money Donna had left for us but, Stephen discovered that, some Months before, she had been putting Money into another account so as to leave us a bit more. Her Lawyer told Stephen about this `secret` account that she had. She had only managed to put £1000 in it before she passed but, again, it showed she was thinking of us.

She was that type of person who preferred giving rather than receiving gifts. I remembered about 5 years before at Christmas; I was on my way to do my Christmas Eve gig at the Loch Awe Hotel. On the way I stopped in at Aldi`s to buy some Juice for my journey. While I was there I noticed that they were selling Kitchen sets of Silver and Black Pots and Pans. I had recently decorated our Kitchen and I remembered Donna say that she was going to get a new Microwave and Toaster. *"I'll get them in Silver and Black,"* she said. Among other Christmas Presents, I had already got her Silver and Black Kitchen utensil set, (Fish turner, Ladle and the like) I was running a bit late so I grabbed the box of Pots and Pans thinking, *"She's going to Love these. She will not be expecting this prezzie"*

I done the gig but, before I left for Home I got some wrapping Paper from the Hotel and wrapped up her `unexpected` gift. After an hour and a half, I arrived back and parked the Car. Walking across the road to our Flat, I looked up to the Christmas Lights at our Window and that brought a wee lump to my throat as it reminded me of when my Daughters used to come and spend Christmas with Donna and I when they were younger. They would sit up with Donna and wait for me getting Home. We would then all sit in a circle on the floor and take turns at opening our presents one at a time.

I always used to run out of Presents first while they each had loads to unwrap.

I got in the House, gave Donna a Christmas Kiss and wished her a Happy Christmas. *"What's that you got there?"* she asked. I said, *"I met Santa at the Hotel and he gave me this Present for you. He said he didn't have room for it on his Sleigh and would I pass it on to you." Nice one, Santa,"* she answered.

Donna got me a Beer from the Fridge and a Glass of Wine for herself. We could not obviously `form a circle` but, we kept up the tradition of sitting on the Floor and opening one Present each. Donna opened her first one. It was a picture of a young teenage Boy and Girl in their Graduation outfits.

"Who's that?" she asked. I said, *"You must know who it is. Who sent you the Present?"* She noticed it was from her Niece, Janette and said, *"Oh. I know who it is now."* Turns out it was the Son and Daughter of Janette. Donna had not seen them since they were little hence why she did not recognize them. I opened my first present, after-shave.

Donna opened her second Present. This one from her Sister, Rita. When I saw what it was, my Heart sank. It was the same Silver and Black Kitchen Utensil set I had bought her.

My turn. Present from Rita, Socks.

Donna's turn. Present from me. Silver and Black Utensil Set, (second one)

My turn. Present from Donna. One share certificate for Celtic Football Club. (She got an extra Kiss for that)

Donna's turn. From me. *"Ah, the Gift that Santa couldn't manage to fit on his Sleigh."* she said. *"I wonder what it is."*

I said that I hope that it made up for me getting her the same Utensil Set as Rita. As soon as she tore off the wrapping, she could see what it was. *"Oh, great"* she said. *"I was going to buy new Pots and* Pans." She opened the top of the box and started to take out the protective wrapping. Bubble wrap, Paper, Cardboard. More Bubble wrap, Paper and Cardboard, and more, and more before realising there was not one Pot or Pan in it.

In my hurry at Aldi`s I had lifted the `Display box`. I thought the box was a bit light when I bought it but I put that down to maybe the material the Pots were made of, and the Girl at the checkout did not seem bothered about its weight.

Donna looked at my `sorry` face and started laughing. *"Whit you like?"* she said. I apologised for being a silly-sod but Donna said, *"I'm not blaming you. I'm blaming that Fat B#####d, Santa."*

The next Morning she got a call from her Friend, Nancy.

Nancy asked her if she was going to make her `Home-made` Steak Pie for Christmas Dinner and, if so, where did you buy the Steak. Donna told her she was indeed making Steak pie and she got the Steak from Phelps the Butcher in Causeyside Street. Nancy told her, *"You'll need to throw the Steak out Donna. A couple of people are* in Hospital with Food Poisoning and it has claimed that it was after eating Meat from Phelps. It might not be but, why take the chance?"

"*Jeez, that's all I need,*" answered Donna. "*This has been some Bloody Christmas.*"

"*What do you mean?*" asked Nancy. And, I must admit, I could not stop laughing when she told Nancy.

"*Wait till Ah tell ye whit ah got for Christmas. Ah got two of the same Present, a picture of people I do not know and an empty F###in` Box.*"

When Donna saw me Laughing, she started Laughing and she said to Nancy, "*Ah well. I'll get Neil to phone his Mum and see if we can go there for Christmas Dinner.*"

I phoned Mum and then said to Donna, "*We can't go to Mums for Dinner*" "*Why not?*" she asked. I said, "*Mum got her Steak from Phelps the Butcher.*"

A day or two after Donna's passing, my

Daughters and I drove up to the Funeral Home on Lady lane where Donna was resting to have one last look at her Beautiful Face. Already there was her Son, Stephen and his Wife, Tanya. My Sisters, Kathleen, Theresa, and Angela, and my Brothers, Joe and Paddy. After about 5 Minutes, they left me alone with Donna. I stood over her open Coffin holding her now Cold Hand and talked to her just an Inch from her Face. I remember a Tear falling from my Eye and landing on Donna's closed Eye. It ran down the side of her Face and looked as though she was the one Crying.

I found it hard to believe that this would be the last I would ever set Eyes on her.

Later that evening my Brothers and Sisters, who had been at the Funeral Home earlier, took me down to the Balnagowan for a few drinks. We sat there remembering Donna and everyone had a story of Donna to tell. Some other Brothers and a Sister also arrived from England throughout the day.

Donna's Sister, Maureen also arrived from Maidenhead.

On the Morning of the Funeral, I had one or two visits to the Flat before the Hearse and Funeral Car arrived. I can remember Paddy got a bit of a fright when he walked into the Living room and saw Donnas Sister sitting in the Chair where Donna always sat. Maureen looked very like Donna only an older version. *"Jeeeeeze-us! "He* shouted. He then got himself together and said, *"Donnas Sister? Right?"*
"How did you guess?" answered Maureen. Paddy whispered to me. *"Nearly shat mahsel`."* I said, *"I know."*
The Hearse arrived and myself, Stephen, Tanya and Granddaughter Victoria, and Maureen, got in the First Car and Nancy, and my Daughters, got in the Second Car. My Brother Joe asked me if I had prepared the Eulogy and would I be okay to read it. I said, *"I wrote and read out Mum and Tony's*

Eulogies. I am the only one who can read out Donna`s.”

As we approached, the Crematorium there was a huge crowd outside. Maureen said, *“That will be the people for Donnas Service. There must be another Service still going on inside.”* It turned out that they were indeed there for Donna`s Service. There was no more room inside as lots of Donnas Friends and old workmates were already inside.

I said to Maureen, *“If I get half as many people at my Funeral, I’ll die a happy man.”* All seats inside were taken and more People standing at the back and all the way out of the Crematorium. She was a much-Loved Person.

After the `Humanist` who hosted the Service had relayed all the nice stories and achievements about Donna`s Life, it was now time for me to read out my Eulogy for Donna.

EULOGY

FOR DONNA

`Where do I start to say how much my Lovely Lady, Donna meant to me? And where do I end?*

Where do I start to say how much my Lovely Lady, Donna meant to her Family? And, where do I end?

And, where do I start to say how much my Lovely Lady, Donna meant to her Friends? Again, where do I end?

She was Funny, Brave, Caring, Beautiful, Loving, and Honest.

Even when fighting off the Grim Reaper, she was more concerned about others like my Sister, Kate, who is still fighting Cancer, and Sister-in-law, Rena who has also been fighting off illness.

She put everyone else before her.

She not only battled with the fact that she had a terminal illness. (She always said she is

living with Cancer and not dying of it).
Some 27 years ago she had to live with the
fact that she had lost her `Wee John`, her
youngest Son in a tragic accident. The worst
thing any Parent could go through.
The Pain of losing her Son never left her.
She was Brave enough to learn to live with it
if only to take care continue to Love her
oldest Son, Stephen who she has always been
so proud of.
She was even brave enough to give
permission to the Hospital to donate her Son
John's organs so as others would benefit
from her loss.

Donna and I had a lovely few years working
and living in Spain but, after some years, she
decided she wanted to return to Paisley.
"WHY?" I asked her. She told me she missed
her Sister, Rita and Friend's, Nancy, June
and many others. She also missed the RAIN,
And, the Botanical Banter she had with my
Dear departed Mother.

Donna changed my Life for the better. She made me realize that LOVE actually existed. She took my three Lovely Daughters under her Wing and was like another Mother to them. She was well named `LOVE`. She made me the Person I am today I know that you will all miss her, especially, Nancy, June, the Beachwood Garden Club members, Son, Stephen and his Wife, Tanya (of whom she was very proud) her Beautiful, Talented Granddaughter, Victoria, Grandson, John and future Grandkid, `the Bump`. I doubt if anyone can miss her more than me. She was my better half in so many ways.

`I dread this Life without you Donna
But, I know where you will be.
From a place where I can't see you,
You'll be watching over me.
I know I'll feel your presence and I will not have to Fear,
I know that you'll be with me, and I will

know that you are near.
So, until the Day we meet again, and I know
that is up above.
I will think of you every single Day, my
Beautiful DONNA LOVE. `

As Stephen and I stood at the exit and thanking people for attending Donnas Farewell, I was amazed at the amount of people that knew Donna. As they were leaving, there was one or two with a smile on their Face because of   Donna's choice of song that was playing on their exit, `*Enjoy yourself. It's later than you think.* ` by Prince Buster. One old Lady said, *"That's Donna for ye."* I asked her what she meant and she Smiled at me and said, *"That song that's playing. Did Donna choose that?"* I told the Lady that she had indeed chose the song. *"Well"* she said, *"that's Donna for ye."*

Chapter 23

I arranged to spend Christmas of 2011 in Bournemouth with my Daughters, as to spend it at Home without Donna would have been unbearable. I'm so lucky to have these Three Lovely and Caring Girls for Daughters.

They helped me through the Festive Season, my first without Donna, and so soon after losing her. It's a difficult time for them also as They lost their Gran, my Mum, just after Christmas of 2009 and their Uncle Tony, my Brother just before Christmas of 2010, not to mention their other Gran and Donna in 2011.

After returning home to Paisley and the wee Flat that had been Home to Donna and I for 13 Years, it was difficult being there on my own. Everywhere I looked, all I could see was Donna in my Mind's Eye. I could smell her Perfume. I could feel her presence but, it wasn't a bad thing. It wasn't just that I was missing her; it was a Comfort in many ways.

One night while lying in Bed I was thinking that the summer is almost here and I should get online and book `our` Holiday back to Icmeler, Turkey. I had to keep my other Promise to Donna.

Later that night as I was drifting off to sleep when my attention was drawn to the Bedroom door. Lots of People have experienced what's known as a `VISIT` from Loved ones that have passed on and swear that it was so vivid it had to be indeed, a Visit.

My experience was so vivid that, to this day, I believe that Donna had paid me a Visit that night.

I looked at the doorway and saw Donna standing and smiling at me. Of course I was confused and somewhat bewildered as I looked at her and said, *"Donna? Donna? What's happening? Are you really here, Babe?"* She just kept Smiling at me and then put her Finger to her Mouth as if to tell me to `hush`. *"I don't have long,"* she said, *"Just letting you know that I am always with you and I will never stop Loving you."* The next thing I knew she was lying beside me but, she had Tears in her Eyes. I asked, *"What's wrong? Why are you crying?* And she answered, *"I miss you, Neil."* I then heard her say, *"Need to go. Love you."* only she was back standing in the doorway again. I looked up and watched her fade away just like you would see in a Ghost Movie. I then realized that I was sitting up in Bed with the Tears running down my Face but, I was smiling. The whole experience was so real, so vivid that I do believe she was with me for those few Minutes.

To this Day I still leave Donna`s side of the Bed available in case she ever decides to pay me another visit.

I know that most of you reading this will put it down to my Grief and missing her so much that my mind played out the scenario of what my sub-conscious mind wished for. That is indeed a possible explanation, and more a scientifically plausible theory but, I will carry on believing that it was real. It gives me Comfort.

I arrived back in Icmeler, Turkey in May of 2012. I booked into the same Hotel where Donna and I had been the year before but, unfortunately not the same room.
I was meant to arrive at 1pm that Day but, because I had been `talked into` having a wee drink the night before with Balnagowan Bar owner, Shirley, I missed my original 07.10am flight. After Shirley went home I decided not to go to Bed so, I just had a Shower and decided to have a Cuppa before phoning a Taxi to the Airport. I put the Kettle on and sat down on the Settee. This was about 05.am. The next thing I knew, it was 07.30am. *"SHIT!!! Missed mah flight."*
I phoned the company I had booked with

and they managed to get me on a later Flight at 7.30pm that night however, it cost me another £90.

I was in my apartment unpacking and had a look out the Balcony. I noticed that the Garden Bar was still open so I headed of for a Beer. Now, I know from living in Mallorca that, although you meet many, many people, you do not remember half of them on their return Holiday but, when I approached the Bar, the Barman looked at me and called out, *"Neil. My good Friend. Great to see you again."* He obviously had a better memory for remembering Tourists than I had when in Mallorca. He came from behind the Bar and greeted me with a Hug. He then said, *"You are looking good my Friend. Where is the Lovely Donna? Is she coming down or is she away to bed?"* I told him of Donna`s passing and he hugged me again saying, *"Sorry, sorry, I'm so sorry my Friend. Donna was a Lovely Lady."* He had a Tear in his Eye and was genuinely upset for me.

It was the same when I went down for Breakfast in the Morning and met `Lucas` the Waiter and Barman. He also recognized me immediately and greeted me with a Hug.

"Good to see you my Friend. Where is the Beautiful Donna?

He reacted in the same way when I told him the Sad news, and was genuinely upset to hear this of his, `Beautiful special Friend` as he called her.

Later that Day I went down for Dinner and Lucas lead me to the Table where Donna and I used to sit the year before. He had laid out table settings for two, and a Bottle of the Wine that Donna had liked with Dinner, and a small Vase of Flowers.

Even the Housemaid had left a `tribute` to Donna by laying Flower Petals on the Bed in the shape of a Heart with an Arrow going through it, and pointing at more Petals in the shape of the letter, `D`.

I scattered some of Donna`s Ashes in the

Hotel Garden where she liked to sit.

I had kept my second promise to Donna. I took her back to Icmeler.

If I ever go back, I will book into the same Hotel. `Hotel Navy, ` it's called.

Chapter 24

My story is probably not much different than the life stories of you who have read this. We all have our stories to tell, some more dramatic, comedic or tragic than mine. We have no choice but to play the cards fate has dealt us.

We are not on this Earth for long so you must try and play those cards in the best way you can.

A means of doing that is to be always nice to others. Keep close to the ones you Love and always be there if you are needed by someone, even a stranger.

You have almost certainly been through some trying times yourself but, you have almost certainly experienced the Love of another. I had quite a good Life until I was 28-years-old but, I had an even better Life since I met Donna.

Unfortunately, she was taken from me far too soon. I will always be grateful for the 30-years I had with Donna but, I wish I had met her 20-years earlier.

I started writing this in 2009, and after writing a couple of chapters, I asked Donna to read it and give me an honest opinion. She was an avid book-reader and also my biggest critic so; I knew she would be nothing less than honest.

She read the chapters I had written, and although I was expecting her to dismiss it, or even at least pull me up on any spelling mistakes, to my pleasant surprise she said, *"That's great, Neil. If it weren't on the monitor screen it would be a page turner. Finish it and get it published."*

I was so happy with her response I couldn't wait to carry on with it.

I took a break from writing after Mum passed away. I hadn't long started back writing it when my Young Brother, Tony also passed away. Donna convinced me to get back on it and, knowing she had limited time left, thanks to Cancer,

She said, *"Keep writing, Neil. Maybe I'll get to read the complete book before it's my turn to go."*

Alas, that was not to be, and after Donna passed I had no interest in finishing `My Story`.

One night last year I came across it and started reading it.

I remembered Donna saying I should finish it and try and get it published. I also thought that by writing about the relationship that Donna and I had, I would have an outlet to tell people about the Love I had, and still have, for her.

I was blessed to have Donna in my life. I'm blessed with Three beautiful Daughters, and Seven Grandkids. I was blessed with two wonderful parents, and twelve loving Siblings. Love is an entity, something that has separate and distinct existence and objective or conceptual reality. It visits almost everyone's life so, treasure it and spread it.

Chapter 25

It seems to be true that you have to pay for everything. You may think that Love costs nothing. Unfortunately, the price you pay for Love is the Grief that you have to endure for the rest of your life when you loose that Love. It is painful and an itch you cannot scratch.

Some of us get by with the belief that when we die, we will be with our lost loved ones again. If you believe that, like I do, then keep believing. If it turns, out not to be true then, at least it has helped you in some way to deal with your Grief and when you die, it will not matter anyway.

I believe that Love is eternal, as is the Soul.
"But what is the Soul?" I hear you ask.
The Soul is akin to the electricity you need
to `bring to life` your Radio, Television,
Computer, and all things that are required
to be `plugged-in`. Otherwise, they are just
empty lifeless vessels, like the vessel known
as your Body. Your Soul is the `electricity`
that makes you `ALIVE`. The organs in
your body, like the Motherboard of your
devices, cannot function without it. You are
`plugged-in` the moment you are conceived.
Well. That is it. I have finished writing `my
story` as I promised Donna I would.
I just hope that there is a Library in Heaven
Love and miss you, Donna. Xxx

So, this is where I say Goodbye but, remember:
"Goodbyes are not for ever'
Goodbyes are not the end. They simply say
`I miss you` Until we meet again."

As for me? I plan to live forever. So far, so good.

Postscript;

Since the loss of my wonderful partner, Donna, I left our home in Paisley and moved to Bournemouth to be near my Daughters and Grandkids. It is great to be able to see them most days as apposed to maybe a week or so once a year.

However, I still miss my Paisley home that I shared with Donna. I moved to Bournemouth a year after Donna is passing Apart from missing my Paisley home, I miss the lovely garden that Donna created out back. I also miss my `local` pub. (I lived above it. You cannot get much more local than that.)

I travelled back to Paisley for a visit in 2016. It was great to catch up with Brothers, Sisters, and friends but I was devastated when I saw what was left of Donna's lovely garden due to neglect. Our neighbours use to say to Donna how lovely she kept the garden and they enjoyed to sit and sunbathe out there in the summer months.
I thought that if they loved it so much they would have at least tried to keep it nice. Maybe even, cut the grass?

Anyway. My book is quite short but, since

writing it, I have remembered many other funny and unusual episodes in my life so, I maybe have to write another.

Take care and may you have more Love, Laughs, and fewer Tears in your life.

Daughters and me.

Mum and Dad.